ESSENTIAL GUIDE TO
FINANCIAL LITERACY FOR KIDS

TURN PASSIVE READING INTO ACTIVE LEARNING WITH REAL-LIFE MONEY SKILLS ON EARNING, SAVING, AND BUDGETING

Copyright © 2025 by Rachael Miller.

All rights reserved.

No portion of this book may be reproduced in any form without written permission from the publisher or author, except as permitted by U.S. copyright law.

This publication is designed to provide accurate and authoritative information in regard to the subject matter covered. It is sold with the understanding that neither the author nor the publisher is engaged in rendering legal, investment, accounting or other professional services. While the publisher and author have used their best efforts in preparing this book, they make no representations or warranties with respect to the accuracy or completeness of the contents of this book and specifically disclaim any implied warranties of merchantability or fitness for a particular purpose. No warranty may be created or extended by sales representatives or written sales materials. The advice and strategies contained herein may not be suitable for your situation. You should consult with a professional when appropriate. Neither the publisher nor the author shall be liable for any loss of profit or any other commercial damages, including but not limited to special, incidental, consequential, personal, or other damages.

Disclaimer

This book, Essential Guide to Financial Literacy for Kids, is intended for educational and entertainment purposes only. It provides general information about financial concepts and does not constitute financial, investment, legal, or professional advice. The content is designed solely to introduce children to financial concepts and should not replace guidance from qualified professionals.

Every effort has been made to ensure the accuracy of the information provided, but the author and publisher offer no warranty or guarantee regarding the accuracy, completeness, or applicability of the content to individual circumstances. Parents and guardians should supervise their children during activities, especially those involving real money or financial decisions.

Interactive activities, quizzes, and games within this book are meant to encourage practical understanding in a safe, supervised environment. Readers are advised to seek professional financial advice for personal financial situations or decisions.

Any mention of specific products, brands, or third-party resources does not imply endorsement by the author or publisher. Readers should independently verify any referenced materials and resources.

By engaging with this book, readers acknowledge and agree to these terms. If you have specific financial questions or need personalized advice, please consult a qualified professional.

Contents

Introduction — 1

Module 1: Money 101 - Understanding the Basics

    1.1 Introduction to Money Basics — 7

    1.2 What is Money — 17

    1.3 Building a Financial Vocabulary — 24

Module 2: The Money Cycle - Earn, Save, Spend Wisely

    2.1 Earning Money: Your First Steps to Financial Independence — 34

    2.2 Saving Money — 41

    2.3 Making Smart Spending Choices — 52

Module 3: Growing Your Wealth - Earning More and Budgeting

    3.1 Ways To Earning More Money — 64

3.2 The Art of Saving   74

3.3 Budgeting Basics for Beginners   84

3.4 Digital Safety in Spending: Smart Choices Online   94

Module 4 - Smart Spending - Making Wise Money Choices

4.1 Taking Saving to the Next Level   104

4.2 Advanced Budgeting Methods   111

4.3 Empowering Financial Independence   120

4.4 Financial Responsibility   129

Module 5: Family Finance Adventures - Lessons For The Whole Family

5.1 Family Financial Fitness   140

5.2 The Family Budget   148

5.3 Family Savings Goal   156

5.4 The Grocery Store Game: Comparing Prices with Famil4   164

5.5 The Financial Quiz: Test Your Money Skill Knowledge!   170

Financial Quiz With Answers!   178

Conclusion   181

References   184

Introduction

When I was a kid, I naturally saved my money, while my younger brother took a very different approach—he spent his money as soon as he got it. I remember carefully setting aside my allowance, watching my savings grow, and feeling proud when I finally had enough to buy something I wanted. Meanwhile, my brother would spend every dollar he had, often on things that didn't last long.

At first, our different money habits didn't seem like a big deal. But as we grew older, I realized how important it was to understand money early. While I had savings to rely on, my brother often found himself short on cash and borrowing money to cover unexpected expenses.

This experience taught me something valuable: **managing money isn't just about saving—it's about planning, budgeting, and making smart financial choices**. When kids learn these skills early, they develop financial confidence that lasts a lifetime. As a mother to two boys, this is important to me.

Why Financial Literacy Matters for Kids

> Did you know that as of 2025, only 21 states require high school students to take a personal finance course?

Millions of kids grow up without basic knowledge about earning, saving, and spending wisely.

But financial literacy isn't just about budgeting—it's about understanding the value of money, setting goals, and making smart choices that help achieve dreams. **I wrote this book—to make learning about money fun, engaging, and easy for kids and families.**

How This Book Works

This book is designed for kids **ages 6-12. It guides** them through financial lessons with **stories, games, activities, and real-life scenarios**. Each module builds on the previous one, starting with simple money concepts and gradually introducing more advanced topics.

How to Use This Book

- **Start Here:** Begin with Module 1 to learn the basics of money.

- **Progress at Your Own Pace**: Move to the next module when comfortable.

- **Complete Fun Activities:** Apply what you learn through quizzes, games, and hands-on challenges.

- **Check the Glossary**– Learn new financial words along the way!

Symbols to Guide You:

Remember: This book is designed to make learning fun! Follow the symbols below to guide your journey. Parents and educators look for "Family Activity" or "Parent Supervision Required" activities to join the adventure and reinforce learning.

What You'll Discover – A preview of the skills and knowledge in each module.

Fun Fact, Tip, Lesson or Entertaining Trivia.

Interactive Activities – Fun ways to practice money skills (quizzes, goal-setting, games).

Key Takeaways – A summary of the most important lessons.

Glossary of Terms– Simple definitions to build financial vocabulary.

Making Learning a Family Experience

Learning about money is **more effective when families are involved**. This book includes activities and prompts for parents and educators to join the learning process.

Family Activity Symbols – Moments where kids can work with parents to reinforce financial lessons

Parent Supervision Required – Sections needing adult guidance, such as opening a savings account or discussing online spending

How Parents Can Reinforce Financial Lessons in Everyday Life

Financial education doesn't have to be complicated—it can be as simple as incorporating money lessons into daily routines! Here are a few ways parents can reinforce what kids learn in this book:

- **Turn Shopping into a Learning Experience** – Let kids compare prices, decide between brands, or calculate discounts.

- **Give Kids Opportunities to Earn Money**—Small jobs, like helping with household tasks, introduce children to work and decision-making.

- **Use Physical Cash When Possible** – Let kids handle real money, count change, and make small purchases.

- **Talk Openly About Money** – Explain everyday financial decisions, like budgeting for groceries or saving for vacations, in a way they understand.

By incorporating small financial lessons into daily life, parents can help children **develop confidence and smart money habits** that will benefit them for years.

Final Thoughts

Money is best learned through real-life practice. This book will guide kids and families on an exciting journey to financial independence, making learning **fun and meaningful.**

Let's get started!

MODULE 1
MONEY 101 - UNDERSTANDING THE BASICS

1.1 Introduction to Money Basics

Welcome to Your Financial Adventure!

Money is all around us! We use it to buy food, toys, and even video games. But do you know where the Money came from? What did people use before coins and bills? Get ready to explore the history of Money and how it helps us every day.

This module introduces the fundamentals of Money—what it is, how it works, and why it's important. Through engaging stories, hands-on activities, and fun discussions, you will explore the history of Money, different forms of Currency, and essential financial habits like saving.

 ## 1.1.1 Learning Objectives

By the end of this module, you will:

- **Understand the basics of Money:** Learn what Money is and why we use it.

- **Explore the history of Money:** See how Money evolved from bartering to modern Currency.

- **Differentiate types of Money:** Coins, bills, and digital Currency.

- **Develop smart money habits:** Practice simple saving strategies through fun activities.

1.1.2 What Is Money? A Fun Journey Through History

Have you ever traded your lunch snack with a friend? You could swap your chocolate chip cookie for a bag of chips. That's called **bartering** – trading one thing for another. But bartering had problems.

What if your friend didn't like cookies? Or what if you wanted something bigger, like a toy or a game? That's why **Money was invented –** to make trading easier! Instead of trading eggs for bread or marbles for a comic book. Let's take an exciting journey through time to see how Money came to be.

The Evolution of Money

Bartering (Trading Goods for Goods)

Long ago, people didn't have Money. If you had extra eggs, you might trade them for what you needed, like bread. But what if the bread-maker didn't need eggs? Bartering could be tricky!

Early Forms of Money (Cowry Shells, Metal Coins)

To solve this problem, early civilizations started using special items such as – **cowry shells, salt, and even cattle**! These items had value because many people wanted them. The first real **metal coins** were made in **Lydia (now Turkey) around 600 BC**. These coins were small, easy to carry, and accepted by everyone, making trade much simpler.

Paper Money and Banks

By **600 AD, China** introduced **paper money**, which was much lighter than carrying coins. Europe started using paper money in the **1600s**. Banks were created to store Money safely.

Modern Money (Digital Currency & Cards)

Today, Money comes in many forms: **coins, paper bills, and digital Currency. We** use **cards, online banking, and digital Currency** to pay for things. We don't always see physical Money, but it still holds value.

1.1.3 Benny's Marketplace Adventure

Before we continue, let's follow Benny on an exciting journey to the marketplace! Let's see what he discovers!

BENNY'S MARKETPLACE ADVENTURE

Once upon a time, a clever young boy named Benny lived in a land filled with excitement and trade. Benny had gathered many acorns to trade at the marketplace. today.

The market around him buzzed with life. With a confident grin, Benny took his first step forward. Benny noticed a baker arranging warm, golden loaves of bread. His stomach rumbled in response. Perfect!

He proudly held up his acorns, offering them with a hopeful smile. The baker chuckled in amusement, then nodded and handed Benny a crusty loaf in exchange. Success! Benny grinned. This trading business wasn't so difficult after all.

Further down the marketplace, Benny saw a beautifully carved wooden horse at the toy stall. His heart leaped—he had to have it. Without hesitation, he offered his loaf of bread. The toy seller studied Benny for a moment, then, with a friendly smile, made the trade.

Benny had traded acorns for bread, and then he traded the bread for a wooden horse. He held the wooden horse in his hands, turning it over with admiration. This was even better than bread!

Feeling confident, Benny approached a fruit stall where fresh apples were neatly piled. Perfect! He held up his wooden horse, anticipating an easy trade. However, the vendor shook their head. "I can't eat a toy," they said with a kind smile. Benny frowned.

"You need money, you can trade for anything without worrying if the other person needs your acorns, bread or a toy." It was Lucy the Coinsmith. She held up a small, gleaming coin. Benny's eyes widened as he listened.

Determined to test his new knowledge, Benny placed a coin in the fruit seller's hand and received a shiny apple in return. Turning to Lucy, he grinned as he took a big, satisfied bite. She nodded in approval.

Today, Benny hadn't just made a trade; he had learned the power of money. He realized that this was the most valuable lesson of all.

Benny's adventure showed us how money helps us get the things we need in a fair way. Just like Benny, we use money to make choices about what to buy and when to save. Now, let's explore why money is so important in our everyday lives!

1.1.4 Why Is Money Important?

Money has three **superpowers** that make life easier:

- **Trade Power**: Money allows us to trade. Instead of bartering, we can simply use money to buy what we need.

- **Value Power**: Money measures value. It helps us compare prices and decide how much something is worth.

- **Future Power**: Money helps us save for the future. Whether in a a piggy bank or a savings account, it allows us to store wealth for future needs.

1.1.5 Understanding Money's Value: Intrinsic vs. Extrinsic

- **Intrinsic Value:** Some things, like gold, are valuable because they are rare and special.

- **Extrinsic Value:** Paper money and coins have value because we all agree they do.
  - Example: If everyone at school decided stickers could be traded for snacks, those stickers would have extrinsic value!)

1.1.6 Money Around the World

Money looks different and has different value in every country! Some countries have colorful bills, while others have coins with unique shapes and images. When traveling, people need to exchange their Money for local Currency. **Exchange rates** tell us how much one country's Money is worth in another country.

Example: If **1 U.S. dollar is equal to 100 Japanese yen**, that means every $1 you have can buy 100 yen worth of goods in Japan.

 ## 1.1.7 Activity – Design Your Own Money!

Now, it's your turn to create your own special Currency!

What You'll Need:

- Paper or cardstock
- Pencils, markers, or crayons
- Scissors (for cutting paper into money shapes)
- Stickers or stencils (optional for extra design)

Step 1: Imagine Your Currency

- What is your currency called? (Example: Star Bucks, Dragon Dollars, Puppy Pesos!)
- Will it be **paper money, coins, or both?**
- What **colors and designs** will you use?
- What **pictures** will be on it? (A pet, a favorite place, or even your face!)
- What **value** will it have? (Example: 1 coin = 5 points in a game)

Step 2: Draw Your Currency

- Draw the front and back of your money.
- Add fun details like patterns and borders.
- Write the value of your currency so others know how much it's worth.

Step 3: Share and Trade!

- Show your currency to friends and family.
- Ask them what they would trade for it!
- Create a pretend store or use it to earn rewards.

1.1.8 Key Takeaways

✔ Money makes trading easier.

✔ Money has **evolved** from bartering to digital payments.

✔ Different countries have different types of money.

✔ Saving money helps us buy important things in the future.

1.1.9 Glossary

- **Bartering** – Trading without money.
- **Digital Currency** – Money used online or through apps.
- **Intrinsic Value** – When something is valuable because it is rare.
- **Extrinsic Value** – When something is valuable because people agree it is.
- **Exchange Rate** – The value of one country's money compared to another's.

Final Thoughts

Money is a powerful tool – it helps us trade, save, and plan for the future. Now that you've learned the basics, you're ready to start using Money wisely! **Up next: What is Money!**

1.2 What is Money

Welcome to an Exciting Journey into the World of Money!

Money comes in many forms—coins, bills, and even digital currency! But what exactly is Money, and how does it help us? In this section, we'll explore the different types of Money and why it plays an essential role in our daily lives.

 ### 1.2.1 Learning Objectives

By the end of this module, you will:

- **Understand the different forms of Money:**
- Coins, bills, and digital transactions.
- **Learn how Money helps** us buy, save, and exchange goods.

- **Discover the differences between physical Money and digital Money.**
- **Develop smart money habits** Through fun activities and games!

1.2.2 Coins, Bills and More!

Imagine a world where superheroes don't wear capes but carry pockets full of coins and bills. **Max Money and Penny Plan** are mighty heroes who will help us understand Money! Together, they show us that Money comes in all shapes and sizes!

Money isn't just numbers—it's a tool that helps us make choices. Whether **buying a tasty treat or saving for something big,** understanding Money is important for making smart decisions.

1.2.3 Coins: Small but Mighty

Coins are small, round, and often shiny metal objects. They come in different sizes and colors. Some coins have smooth edges, while others have ridges. Each type of coin—pennies, nickels, dimes, and quarters—has its own value and design. They may be tiny, but they hold great power!

1.2.4 Activity – Fun with Coins!

Coin Exploration

- Ask a parent or guardian for a variety of coins.
- Spread them out and examine their designs—what do you notice?
- Play **"Guess the Coin"**: One person describes a coin, and the other guesses which one it is!

Coin Rubbing Art!

Coins have unique designs, and you can uncover them with a fun art activity!

What You'll Need:

- Coins of different sizes and values
- A sheet of paper
- Crayons (lighter colors work best)

Steps 1

Gather different coins and place them on a flat surface.

Steps 2

Lay a sheet of paper over the coins.

Steps 3

Take a crayon and gently rub it over the paper where the coins are placed.

Steps 4

Watch as the coin's design appears like magic!

Steps 5

Try using different colors to make your artwork more vibrant.

Bonus Challenge!

- Arrange your coin rubbings into a fun collage.
- Label each rubbing with the coin's name and value.
- Try doing rubbings with foreign coins or special edition coins if you have them.

1.2.5 Bills: Money on Paper!

Unlike coins, **bills** are lightweight and fold easily into wallets. Each bill has a number that tells its value, from **$1 to $100**. Bills often have pictures of famous people and landmarks, making them like **miniature history books!**

 Fun Fact – Did you know some countries use plastic for their bills instead of paper?

1.2.6 Activity – Money Detective!

1. Grab a magnifying glass and examine different bills.

2. Look for hidden details like watermarks and security features.

3. Discuss with a friend or family member—why do money designs include these details?

1.2.7 Digital Currency: The Future of Money!

In the modern world, Money doesn't just exist as coins and bills—it also lives **inside computers and smartphones!** This is called **digital currency**.

What is Digital Money?

Instead of exchanging physical Money, we can pay online using:

- **Bank apps**
- **Credit and Debit cards**

- **Digital wallets (like Apple Pay, Google Pay, or PayPal)**

Example: Have you ever bought an app or a game online? That's **digital Money in action!**

> **Understanding Cryptocurrencies** Cryptocurrencies like **Bitcoin** are a special type of digital Money. Unlike regular Money from a bank, cryptocurrencies are stored securely online. Don't worry if this sounds tricky—you'll learn more about it when you're ready!

 1.2.8 Key Takeaways

✔ **Coins and bills** help us buy and trade.

✔ **Digital Money** is becoming more common.

✔ **Money has changed over time, but its purpose stays the same!**

✔ **Learning how to use Money wisely is an important life skill!**

 **1.2.9 Glossary of Terms**

- **Bartering** – Trading goods or services without using Money.

- **Coins** – Small, round metal pieces used as Money.

- **Bills** – Paper money that represents different

amounts of value.

- **Digital Currency** – Money that exists electronically and can be used for online purchases.

- **Bank** – A place where people keep their Money safe.

- **Digital Wallet** – An app that stores and uses Money online.

- **Savings** – Money set aside for future use.

- **Budget** – A plan that helps people decide how to spend and save Money.

- **Interest** – Extra Money earned when you save in a bank.

- **Cryptocurrency** – A special type of digital Money that isn't controlled by banks.

Final Thoughts

Money is more than just paper and coins—it's a tool that helps us **trade, save, and plan for the future.** Now that you've learned about different forms of Money, you're one step closer to becoming a **money-smart hero!**

1.3 Building a Financial Vocabulary

A Treasure Hunt for Money Words!

Have you ever been on a treasure hunt? Imagine finding a map with clues leading to a chest filled with shiny coins and sparkling gems. **Building a financial vocabulary is a little bit like that treasure hunt.** The words you learn are your clues, and the treasure is the wisdom you gain from understanding money. Like a detective, you can define each term and discover how it fits into your life.

 ## 1.3.1 Learning Objectives

By the end of this module, you will:

- **Understand key financial terms:** Income, expense, savings, and budget.

- **Recognize how these terms apply:** Use them in

real-life money decisions.

- **Learn to track and manage money effectively.**
- **Create a personal finance dictionary:** Build your financial knowledge.
- **Engage in fun activities:** Make learning money words exciting!

Knowing these words makes you smarter with money and helps you make better choices. Let's dive into some important money terms to help you on your treasure hunt!

1.3.2 Word Wise: Understanding Common Money Terms

Income

Income is like the treasure you earn from your adventures. When you do chores, receive an allowance, or earn money from a small job, that's your **Income**. Think of it as the coins that come to you as a reward for your hard work and effort. You can **save** it, **spend** it, or **plan for something big**!

Expense

An **expense** is the money you spend to buy what you need or want—like a snack, a toy, or school supplies. Every time you purchase something, you use your Income to cover an expense. **Keeping an eye on your expenses helps you stay on course toward your savings goals.**

Savings

Savings are the money you set aside for the future. Imagine keeping part of your treasure safe for later use. Maybe you're saving for a new game, a bike, or a fun trip. **Every time you put money in your piggy bank or savings account, you grow your treasure chest!**

> **Fun Fact – When you keep money in a bank, they might give you extra money called 'interest' as a reward for saving!**

Budget

A **budget** is your map for a financial treasure hunt. It shows you **where your money will go** and helps you decide **how much to save and spend**. A budget keeps you on track to reach your financial goals!

1.3.3 Activity – Create Money Flashcards!

What You'll Need:

- Index cards or paper
- Markers or crayons

Steps:

1. **On one side** – Draw a picture representing **income,**

expense, savings, and budget.

2. **On the other side** – Write the definition.

Example:

- Draw a **piggy bank** for "savings."
- Draw a **toy store** for "expense."
- Draw a **chore list with dollar signs** for "income."
- Draw a **map with coins** for "budget."
- Use your flashcards to **test yourself** or play a game with friends!

1.3.4 Activity – Exploring Financial Terms in Your Daily Life

Term Treasure Hunt!

Look for real-life examples of **Income, expenses, savings, and budgeting at home!**

Find:

- A **grocery receipt** (expense)
- A **piggy bank or savings jar** (savings)
- A **list of chores with payments** (income)
- A **weekly allowance plan** (budgeting)

 **Discuss with your family** how each item fits into your financial treasure hunt!

Play: "Term Charades"!

Pick a financial term and **act it out** while others try to guess it.

Example: Pretend to **buy something** for "expense" or pretend to **save coins** in a piggy bank for "savings."

1.3.5 The Finance Dictionary: Creating Your Own Glossary

Imagine having a **special notebook** as your **finance dictionary**. You can **write down new money words and their meanings** in this place. This will be **your personal glossary** to help you understand and remember financial terms.

Get Started!

- Grab a **notebook** or **some sheets of paper**
- Write down terms like **savings, budget, expense, and Income**
- Add simple definitions in **your own words**
- Write an **example sentence** to show how the Word is used in real life.
- Draw small pictures to help remember each Word!

Make It Fun! Use **color coding**:

- Blue for savings
- Green for income
- Red for expenses

Add **stickers or doodles** that make learning enjoyable!

Glossary Template

My Personal Finance Glossary

Word #1: _____

Definition: _____
Example Sentence: _____
Draw a picture: (Use this space to draw a fun illustration!)

 ## 1.3.6 Key Takeaways

✔ **Income** is the money you earn.

✔ **Expenses** is the money you spend.

✔ **Savings** help you prepare for future goals.

✔ **A budget** helps you plan how to use your money wisely.

✔ **Building your financial vocabulary** makes you smarter with money!

 ## 1.3.7 Glossary of Terms

- **Income** – Money you earn from work, chores, or allowance.

- **Expense** – Money you spend on things you need or want.

- **Savings** – Money set aside for the future.

- **Budget** – A plan for how to use your money wisely.

- **Interest** – Extra money earned when saved in a bank.

- **Investment** – Using money to grow more money over time.

- **Bank** – A place to keep your money safe.

Final Thoughts

Understanding money terms is like **unlocking secret treasures** that help you **become a money-smart hero**. Keep learning new words, using them in real life, and growing your financial skills. **Each Word is a step toward making smarter choices and achieving your money goals!**

> **Keep Going, You're Doing Great!**
>
> If something doesn't make sense right away, that's okay! Learning about money takes time.
>
> You can:
>
> - **Review any part of any Module or Section**
> - **Ask a parent or teacher for help**
> - **Try hands-on activity to practice!**
>
> Every step you take brings you closer to becoming a money-smart pro. Don't forget to check the glossary for new words. Most importantly, **have fun and enjoy your journey to financial confidence!**

Transition to Module 2: Earning, Saving and Smart Spending

Now that you've mastered the basics of money—what it is, how it works, and the key terms that help you understand it—let's take the next step in your financial journey! In **Module 2**, we'll explore how people earn money, the value of hard work, and exciting ways to start earning money yourself. Get ready to discover new opportunities and learn how to make your money grow!

MODULE 2
THE MONEY CYCLE - EARN, SAVE, SPEND WISELY

2.1 Earning Money: Your First Steps to Financial Independence

Welcome to Module 2!

Now that you understand what Money is and how it is used, it's time to learn how to **earn and save**. In this module, you'll explore **different ways to make Money, the importance of saving, and how to make smart financial decisions**.

 ### 2.1.1 Learning Objectives

By the end of this section, you will:

- Understand different ways people **earn Money**.
- Learn about **hard work, skills, and effort** in earning Money.
- Discover ways **kids can earn Money**.

- Differentiate between **active and passive income**.

2.1.2 How Do People Earn Money?

People earn Money by working in different jobs. Some jobs require **special skills**, like doctors, engineers, or artists who train for many years, while others need **hard work and practice**, such as construction workers, chefs, and farmers. Some people work for **companies** with set schedules and pay. In contrast, others start their own **businesses** and become entrepreneurs, creating products or services for others. **No matter the job, earning Money takes effort, responsibility, and dedication!**

Examples of Jobs

- **A doctor** helps sick people.
- **A teacher** helps kids learn.
- **A chef** makes tasty meals.
- **A truck driver** delivers packages.
- **A shop owner** sells things to people.

List 3 jobs you think would be fun. What do people in those jobs do?

2.1.3 Earning Money as a Kid

Even kids can earn Money! Imagine you're on a grand adventure, searching for treasure. But instead of a pirate ship and hidden gold, **your treasure comes from the Money you earn** through hard work and creativity.

Earning Money can be **exciting and rewarding.** You don't need a pirate map or an island—your journey starts at home. You can **earn by helping with household chores**, setting up a lemonade stand, or using your creativity to make things to sell. Every task is like a mini-quest, where the coins you earn reward for your effort.

Hard work pays off! The more effort you put into tasks, the more rewards you earn. This doesn't just apply to earning Money—it's a life skill that helps in school, sports, and hobbies.

And don't forget about special occasions! **Birthday money and gifts** can be great ways to grow your savings. Instead of spending everything at once, think about setting aside a portion for something important or saving for a future goal. **Thoughtful spending and saving will help you build strong money habits.**

Do you want to know the best part about earning your own Money? **You are in control.** You decide how much **effort** you put into earning Money and what to do with it. Will you save it for something special, spend it on something you love, or invest it in a new idea? Every decision teaches valuable lessons about responsibility and money management.

2.1.4 Earning money through Chores

Let's look at how you can start earning Money as a Kid. Many families have a system where kids can earn an allowance or pocket money by completing chores. Think of chores as small jobs that help your home run smoothly. Each completed job earns you Money and helps build your sense of responsibility.

Examples of Chores for Earning Money:

Simple Chores (Ages 6-8):

- Making your bed
- Picking up toys
- Helping set the table
- Watering plants

Turn chores into exciting adventures! You can choose tasks that fit your skills and interests using a chore chart, turning responsibilities into challenges with rewards!

2.1.5 Activity – Chore Chart System for Kids

Turn Chores into Exciting Adventures!

What You'll Need:

- A **chart or board** (paper or dry-erase board works well)
- Stickers, markers, or colored pens
- A container to collect earned rewards (coins, tickets, or stars)

How to Use Your Chore Chart

Step 1: Choose Your Chores

Discuss with parents to pick chores that match your abilities. Here are some examples:

- **Tidy your room** – Organize toys and make your bed.
- **Take out the trash** – Conquer the garbage heap!
- **Sweep the floor** – Keep the castle clean!
- **Help set the table** – Prepare for a royal feast!
- **Feed a pet** – Take care of your loyal companion.

Step 2: Track Your Progress

- Write down the chores on your chart.
- Each time you complete a chore, **place a sticker or checkmark** next to it.

Step 3: Earn and Save!

- Each completed chore earns you **pocket money** or a special token.
- **Save your earnings** and decide how to use them wisely.
- **Learn to budget** by choosing when to spend and when to save!

Bonus Challenge!

- Set a **family challenge** where everyone competes to earn the most rewards in a week.

- Create a **"Chore Marketplace"** where chores have different values, and you can pick which ones to complete for greater rewards.

- Try a **team chore** where you and a sibling or friend work together and **share the reward!**

2.1.6 Active vs. Passive Income

There are **two main ways** people earn money: **active income** and **passive income**.

Understanding Different Types of Income

- **Active Income:** You work to earn money (e.g., doing chores for an allowance).

- **Passive Income:** You earn money over time with little ongoing effort (e.g., selling handmade bracelets online).

Understanding these two types of income can help you think of creative ways to earn Money, even when you're not actively working. Many adults build passive income streams to create financial security.

2.1.7 Key Takeaways

✔ **Earning** money requires **effort and responsibility.**

✔ Completing tasks gives a **sense of accomplishment.**

✔ **Managing earnings** wisely is an **important life skill.**

✔ Active income **requires working for money,** while passive income continues earning with less effort over time.

2.1.8 Glossary

- **Earning:** Receiving money for work done.
- **Chore Chart:** A visual tracker for tasks and rewards.
- **Active Income:** Money earned by working (like chores or small jobs).
- **Passive Income:** Money earned with little ongoing effort (like selling digital products or handmade crafts).

Final Thoughts

Earning money is an **exciting journey** that teaches responsibility, effort, and financial wisdom. Whether through **chores, small jobs, or creative ideas**, learning how to earn helps you take control of your financial future.

2.2 Saving Money

The Magic of Saving

Saving money is like planting seeds that grow into something great. Imagine three little pigs:

- **Saver Pig** stores acorns for the future.
- **Spender Pig** spends his acorns as soon as he gets them.
- **Planner Pig** balances saving and spending wisely.

When a storm arrives, Saver Pig and Planner Pig are ready, while Spender Pig struggles because he didn't save. Just like these pigs, **you can choose how to manage your money**. A great way to start is using a **Savings Jar or Piggy Bank**. Label it with your goal and watch your savings grow over time. **Every coin saved brings you closer to something special, whether it's a new toy or a fun trip!**

 ## 2.2.1 Learning Objectives

By the end of this section, you will:

- Understand the **importance of saving money.**
- Learn different ways to **save**.
- Set personal **savings goals**.
- Set financial goals to help **manage money wisely**.
- **Understand why celebrating savings milestones is important.**
- **Learn how to reflect on what helped you succeed.**

2.2.2 Piggy Banks and Savings Jars: Starting Your Own Savings

Saving money might seem simple, but it's a powerful skill that helps you prepare for the future. Think about this: if you spend all your money the moment you get it, what happens when you really want something special, like a new game or a trip to an amusement park? You might not have enough! That's why saving is important—it allows you to plan for exciting things ahead instead of feeling stuck when you don't have enough money. Not saving can lead to disappointment when you can't afford something you really want.

When you save money, you make a smart decision for your future self. Imagine finding a jar filled with coins and bills when you least expect it—how exciting would that be? When you put money away little by little, you create your own surprise fund for future adventures! There are different ways to save money, and choosing a method that works for you makes saving easier and more fun. One of the best ways to start is using a **piggy bank or a savings jar**. These act like treasure chests where you store your money safely until you can use it for something important.

A **piggy bank** is a fun, classic way to store money. Every time you drop a coin inside, you hear the clink and know you're one step closer to your goal. A **savings jar** is another great option because it's clear—you can actually see your savings grow! Watching your money pile up is a great motivation to keep going.

Saving isn't just about keeping your money; it's about making choices. Each time you receive money, you have three options:

1. **Spend it** – Buy something fun right away.
2. **Save it** – Keep it for a bigger goal.
3. **Share it** – Give some to a good cause or help others.

A good balance of these choices helps you become responsible with money. And don't forget—you can decorate your savings jar or piggy bank to make it special and uniquely yours! A piggy bank or savings jar acts like a **treasure chest**, where you store money for future goals. **Start with a simple strategy:**

"Save a Little, Gain a Lot."

Set **aside a portion of each paycheck for savings**. Over time, small savings add up, helping you reach your goal.

> **Fun Fact – A piggy bank is sturdy and fun, and it makes a satisfying clink when you drop a coin in. A savings jar is clear, so you can see your money grow! Decorate your jar to make it uniquely yours.**

2.2.3 Activity – Savings Jar Activity

Watch Your Savings Grow!

A savings jar is a great way to see your money grow over time. This hands-on activity makes saving money exciting and rewarding.

What You'll Need:

- A **clear jar** with a lid
- Stickers, markers, or paint for decoration
- A **label** for your savings goal
- **Coins and bills** to start saving

Step 1 – Personalize Your Savings Jar

Find a clear jar so you can **see your savings grow**. Use stickers, paints, or markers to decorate it with fun designs.

Label your jar with your savings goal, like **"New Toy Fund"** or **"Adventure Money."**

Step 2 – Start Saving!

Each time you receive money, **decide how much to add** to your jar. Watch your savings increase as you add more!

Step 3 – Learn and Reflect

Think about how saving helps you **reach your goals**. Discuss how long it might take to save for something special.

Bonus Challenge!

- **Set up different jars** for different goals (**spending, saving, giving**).
- **Create a savings chart** to track how much you add each week.
- **Challenge yourself** to save a little extra each time you get money!

2.2.4 My First Savings Goal: From Dream to Reality

Now that we know how to save, let's consider **why** we save money.

Story Time: Ella's Ice Cream Dream

Ella loved ice cream more than anything and wanted to buy a **giant ice cream cone** with sprinkles. Her mom said she could but had to **save her coins first**.

Ella began by putting all her spare change into a jar. Every day, she added a few more coins and **counted them often,** practicing her math skills. Finally, the day arrived when **Ella had enough coins.** She proudly marched to the ice cream shop and **bought their biggest cone.** Her hard work and savings had paid off!

Now, **think about something you really want to buy.** In the past, you would have asked your parents to buy it for you. But now you've earned some money and **can take control and buy it yourself. How empowering is that?**

Okay, so you're wondering: What if it costs more than what you have saved? Don't worry! This is where setting a **savings goal** comes into play. By setting a specific target, like saving for that toy you want, you now have a savings goal. Each coin you save brings you closer to buying the item you desire, and it's a great way to stay focused and determined.

In Ella's story, she had a goal of buying ice cream. She saved her coins over many days, carefully watching and counting as her collection grew. It's like climbing a staircase; each step represents a small part of your big dream. Having a savings goal and tracking your progress is a great way to see where you started and how far you've come.

 **Steps to Achieve Your Savings Goal:**

1. **Pick Your Goal** – What are you saving for? **(Example: A new book, a toy, or a fun trip!)**

2. **Set a Savings Target** – Find out how much it costs.

3. **Break It Down** – Save a little each week instead of all at once.

4. **Track Your Progress** – Use a chart, savings ladder, or color in a picture as you get closer to your goal.

5. **Celebrate!** – When you reach your goal, **enjoy your reward!**

Bonus Activity: Share your goal with a family member or friend! They can cheer you on and **help keep you motivated!**

2.2.5 Activity – Create Your Own Goal-Tracking Poster!

What You Need:

- Paper or poster board
- Markers, crayons, or colored pencils
- Stickers, stamps, or small decorations (optional)
- Ruler or something to help draw straight lines (optional)

How to Make Your Poster:

Step 1: Pick Your Goal

Think of something you want to save for.
Example: **"I want to save $20 for a new book."**

Step 2: Draw Your Goal in the Center

On your paper, **draw a big picture of your goal** in the center. You can also cut out or print a picture to paste on your poster.

Step 3: Create a Path to Your Goal

Draw a **fun path** leading to your goal. (**straight road, winding trail, staircase, stepping stones across a river**).

Make sure to leave space for **checkpoints along the way!**

Step 4: Add Checkpoints for Savings Milestones

Each checkpoint is a small step toward reaching your goal. **Example:** If your goal is $20, your checkpoints might be:

- $5 saved / $10 saved / $15 saved / $20 saved – GOAL REACHED!

Step 5: Decorate Your Poster

Make your goal tracker **fun and exciting!** Use colors, stickers, or doodles. Write words of encouragement like **"I can do it!"** or **"Keep saving!"**

Step 6: Track Your Progress

Every time you save money, mark your progress!

- **Color in the path as you go**
- **Place a sticker at each checkpoint**
- **Cross off amounts as you reach them**

Step 7: Celebrate When You Reach Your Goal!

Once you reach the last checkpoint, **celebrate your success! Buy the item or experience you saved for.** Start thinking about your next savings goal!

2.2.6 Why We Need to Celebrate

Saving money takes time, effort, and smart decision-making. When you finally reach your goal, whether it's buying a new toy, saving for a trip, or simply building up your savings, it's important to **celebrate your success!** Acknowledging your achievements makes you feel proud, builds confidence, and keeps you motivated to reach even bigger goals in the future.

Think of it like finishing a big race or completing a difficult puzzle—seeing all your hard work pay off is exciting! Let's explore fun ways to **celebrate financial milestones** and make saving money even more rewarding.

2.2.7 Reflect and Celebrate Achievements

Take a moment to celebrate your achievements and reflect on what helped you succeed.

Consider keeping a **Success Journal** to write down your thoughts. Here are some journal prompts to get you started:

- What was the most challenging part about saving money?
- What did you do to stay committed to your goal?
- How did you feel when you finally reached your savings target?

- "What will I save for next?"

2.2.8 Key Takeaways

✔ **Saving money** helps you prepare for the future.

✔ **Using a piggy bank or savings jar** makes saving fun.

✔ Setting a **savings goal keeps you motivated.**

✔ **Tracking progress** helps you stay on course.

✔ Celebrating **savings milestones** keeps you motivated.

✔ **Reflecting** on success helps you learn from your experience.

2.2.9 Glossary

- **Savings** – Money set aside for future use.
- **Savings Goal** – Something you plan to save money for.
- **Budget** – A plan for how to spend and save money.
- **Savings Jar** – A container to collect and track your savings.
- **Milestones** – Small steps that help track progress toward a goal.
- **Success Journal** – A journal where you reflect on your progress and goals.

Final Thoughts

Saving money is **one of the best habits you can develop!** Whether you're saving for a special toy, a big adventure, or just planning ahead, learning to save helps you make smart choices. Celebrating your savings success **makes the journey fun** and helps you stay excited about reaching new goals.

Keep saving, keep celebrating, and keep achieving amazing things!

2.3 Making Smart Spending Choices

The Power of Smart Spending

Spending money is easy, but **spending wisely** is a skill that takes practice. Every time you buy something, you're making a choice. Do you buy a new toy, save your money for something bigger, or spend it on a snack that will be gone in minutes? **Making smart spending choices helps you get the most out of your money!**

Have you ever bought something and later wished you had saved your money for something else? This is why thinking before you spend is so important. Smart spending means making decisions that you **won't regret later**, and that help you reach your financial goals. Let's learn how to make better choices!

 ## 2.3.1 Learning Objectives

What You'll Learn in This Module:

- Understand the difference between **needs and wants.**
- Learn how to make better **spending decisions.**
- Use tools like **"The Spending Checklist"** to think before buying.
- Practice sorting and prioritizing **spending choices.**

2.3.2 Understanding Needs vs. Wants

Understanding the difference between **needs and wants** is like having a **map for your money**. It helps you **navigate your choices** so you can spend wisely and reach your financial goals faster.

What Are Needs and Wants?

- **Needs** are things you must have to live. These include **food, clothing, shelter, transportation, and school supplies**. Without these things, life would be very difficult.
- **Wants** are things that are nice to have but **aren't necessary for survival**. These include **toys, candy, video games, trendy clothes, and fast food.**

Why Is It Important to Know the Difference?

Many people struggle with money because they spend too much on wants and don't have enough for their needs. **When you understand the difference, you can make better choices and feel in control of your money!** Think about what happens if you **spend all your money on wants** before paying for your needs. What if you buy a bunch of candy and then don't have enough for a warm jacket when winter comes? Learning to **balance spending on needs and wants** is key to becoming a smart spender.

Let's look at Anna's story.

Meet Anna! Anna had saved up some allowance money. She wanted to buy candy but also had her eye on a toy she'd wanted for a long time.

Anna thought about her choices:

- The candy would be gone quickly.
- The toy would last much longer and bring her joy for weeks.

She **chose the toy** and felt proud of her decision!

Understanding the difference between needs and wants **helps you become a wise spender and a happier saver!**

Making smart spending choices isn't just about saving money—it's about **feeling good about your decisions** and making sure your money goes to things that truly matter.

2.3.3 Activity – Need – Wants Sorting

What You Need:

- A stack of **index cards** or small pieces of paper
- A **marker** or pen
- Two **bowls, envelopes, or labeled areas** for sorting

Step 1: Write Down Items

On each card, write different things you might want to buy or spend money on. Examples:

- Pizza
- Toy car
- Jacket
- Chocolate bar
- School supplies
- New shoes

Step 2: Sort into Needs and Wants

Take your cards and **decide if each item is a need or a want**. Place them into two separate piles or labeled bowls.

Step 3: Discuss with a Family Member

- Why did you sort each item the way you did?
- Are there some items that could be **both a need and a want**?
- How can understanding the difference help you make smart money choices?

Step 4: Reflect and Set Priorities

- Look at your needs and wants list.
- If you have a savings goal, consider whether you might want to adjust your spending to focus more on needs first.

2.3.4 Think Before You Buy

Have you ever bought something and later wished you **hadn't**? Maybe you spent all your money on a new game, only to realize later that you needed a new backpack for school. **That's why thinking before you buy is so important!**

When you pause and ask yourself a few key questions before making a purchase, you can avoid **impulse buying** and make sure your money is going toward things that truly matter. **A Spending Checklist helps you slow down and make smart financial choices.**

Why Use a Spending Checklist?

- It **prevents impulse buying** (buying things without thinking first).

- It helps you **save money** for important things.

- It makes sure you **won't regret your spending choices later**.

- It helps you **prioritize your needs over wants**.

 ## 2.3.5 Activity – The Spending Checklist

Before making any purchases, **empower yourself** with "The Spending Checklist." This simple tool helps you take control of your spending and avoid impulse buying.

Using "The Spending Checklist" helps build smart money habits and thoughtful decision-making!

Step 1: Ask Yourself Before Buying

- **Do I really need this?**

- **Will this make me happy in the long run?**

- **Is there something else I need more?**

- **Can I afford it without using all my savings?**

- **Have I compared prices or looked for deals?**

Example: Imagine you see a cool new toy at the store. You're excited and want to buy it right away! But wait—before you spend, use the **Spending Checklist**:

- Do I need this? **No, it's a want.**

- Will it make me happy for a long time? **Maybe, but it could also get boring after a week.**

- Is there something I need more? **Yes, I need to save for a school field trip.**

- Can I afford it without using all my savings? **No, it would take up most of my money.**

- Have I checked if there's a better price somewhere else? **No, I could look for a sale or a secondhand option.**

Using the checklist, you realize it's better to wait and think about whether you truly want the toy. This helps you make a smarter spending choice!

Step 2: Practice with Role-Playing

Pretend you're in a store with a limited budget.

- Look at different items and **decide what you would buy.**

- Discuss with a family member **why you made those choices.**

- Think about **what you might do differently next time.**

Step 3: Reflect on Your Spending Habits

- **Keep track of things** you wanted to buy but didn't.
- **Look at past purchases**—did they bring lasting happiness?
- **Make a list of future items** you truly need versus those you want.

2.3.6 Key Takeaways

✔ **Knowing the difference between needs and wants** helps you make better spending choices.

✔ **Thinking before buying** prevents regret and keeps you on track with your savings goals.

✔ **Using "The Spending Checklist"** helps you pause and reflect before making a purchase.

✔ **Prioritizing what truly matters** allows you to use your money wisely and feel good about your choices!

2.3.7 Glossary

- **Needs** – Things necessary for living, like food and clothes.
- **Wants** – Things that are nice to have but not necessary, like toys or candy.
- **Impulse Buying** – Buying something without thinking

about it first.

- **Prioritizing** – Deciding what is most important.

- **Spending Checklist** – A tool to help you decide if a purchase is a smart choice.

Final Thoughts

Making smart spending choices **isn't about saying no to fun things—it's about making sure your money goes to what truly matters**. When you think before you buy, you'll have more money for things that make a real difference in your life!

Keep learning, keep practicing, and keep making smart money choices!

Keep Going!

If something doesn't make sense right away, that's okay! You can:
- **Review a section or Module**
- **Ask a parent or teacher for help**
- **Try any of the hands-on activity**

Every step you take brings you closer to being a money-smart pro! **Keep learning, exploring, and having fun with money!**

Transition to Module 3: Saving & Budgeting

Now that you've explored the many ways to **earn money**—whether by helping out at home, starting a small business, or taking on small jobs—it's time to take the next step in your financial journey!

In **Module 3**, we'll dive into **saving and budgeting**, two of the most important money skills you'll ever learn. You'll discover how to **set savings goals**, make **smart spending choices**, and build a budget that helps you manage your money wisely.

Get ready to learn how to **make your money work for you** and reach your financial goals faster!

MODULE 3
GROWING YOUR WEALTH - EARNING MORE AND BUDGETING

3.1 Ways To Earning More Money

Level Up Your Earning Power!

You're now ready for advanced challenges! In **Module 3**, you'll discover ways to **boost your earning power** and make **smart spending choices**. Activities here will test your **skills and creativity**, like starting your own small business or planning a **family savings challenge!**

 ### 3.1.1 Learning Objectives

By the end of this section, you will:

- **Explore new ways to earn money beyond chores.**
- **Learn how responsibility leads to more earnings.**
- **Discover how to turn hobbies and skills into income.**
- **Understand the basics of entrepreneurship.**

3.1.2 Building Earning Power

Did you know that building your earning power is about more than just making money? It's about learning **responsibility, independence, and decision-making skills** that will help you throughout life! By expanding what you already do, you can increase your earning potential and **make your money grow faster!**

Expanding Your Chore List

Chores aren't just about helping at home—they're **your first job**! If you've already been doing small tasks, it's time to take on **bigger responsibilities** that can help you earn more. The secret? The **more valuable the task, the more money you can negotiate!**

For example, consider the difference between picking up toys and helping prepare dinner. One takes a few minutes, while the other is a skill you can build and use throughout life. **The more effort and responsibility a chore takes, the more valuable it becomes!**

Here are some advanced chores that can help you earn more:

Daily Chores:

- Make your bed

- Brush your teeth & get dressed (morning/evening routine) - Self care is and important Life Skill

- Put dirty clothes in the laundry hamper

- Pick up toys and personal items

- Set and clear the table for meals
- Wipe down counters and tables after meals
- Water houseplants

Weekly Chores:

- Vacuum or sweep small areas
- Take out the trash (small bins)
- Change bed sheets with assistance
- Help care for pets (feeding, brushing, refilling water)
    - This shows you're responsible and trustworthy.
- Wipe down the car interior (dust the dashboard, pick up trash)
- Pull weeds or help in the garden

Chores with Supervision:

- Sort laundry (whites vs. colors)
- Load/unload the dishwasher
- Help prepare meals (washing vegetables, mixing ingredients) – Learning to cook is an important life skill.
- Clean bathroom sink and mirrors
- Take a short walk with a younger sibling or pet – This shows you're responsible and trustworthy.

Negotiation Tip: Sit down with your parents and ask, **"What extra chores can I do to earn more?"** Work out a plan together so that both sides are happy.

3.1.3 The Importance of Quality Work

Did you know that **how well you do a job** is just as important as getting it done? **Quality work** makes people trust you, recommend you to others, and even offer you better opportunities in the future.

Imagine this: You get paid to rake leaves, but instead of collecting them neatly, you leave some behind, and the wind blows them back into the yard. Your neighbor might not ask you to do it again! But if you take your time and do the job properly, they'll be impressed and may even offer you more work.

Why Quality Work Matters

✔ **Earns trust** – When you do a good job, people will want to hire you again.

✔ **Leads to more opportunities** – Satisfied customers might recommend you to friends and family.

✔ **Teaches responsibility** – Taking pride in your work builds strong habits for the future.

✔ **Increases your earnings** – Some people will **pay more** for a job well done!

Example: Alex Learns the Value of Quality Work

Alex wanted to earn money cleaning garages. At first, he rushed through the job, sweeping quickly without organizing the tools. His customer wasn't happy and didn't ask him back. Next time, Alex took his time, sorted everything neatly, and even wiped down surfaces. **His customer was so impressed that they gave him a bonus and recommended him to their friends!**

Quality work = More trust and more earnings!

By focusing on quality, you'll build a **great reputation** and earn **even more money** in the long run!

Tips for Doing Quality Work

- **Take your time** – Rushing leads to mistakes.

- **Double-check your work** – Look over everything to make sure it's done properly.

- **Ask for feedback** – See if your customer is happy or if anything can be improved.

- **Go the extra mile** – Doing a little extra can make a big difference!

3.1.4 The Entrepreneurship of Earning

Have you ever dreamed of **being your own boss**? Entrepreneurs create their own ways to earn money by solving problems and offering valuable services. Instead of waiting for an allowance, you can start a **small business** and control your income!

Think about what people around you **need or want**. You have the perfect business idea if you can **offer something helpful or unique**!

Turning Everyday Skills into Business Ideas

Every skill or hobby can be turned into an income stream if you **think outside the box!** Here are some fun ideas:

- **Design & Sell T-Shirts** – Create cool designs and sell them online or at school events.

- **Craft & Sell Handmade Goods** – Friendship bracelets, painted rocks, or bookmarks!

- **Pet Sitting or Dog Walking** – Help neighbors care for their pets.

- **Tutoring Younger Kids** – Teach subjects you love, like math or reading.

- **Gardening & Lawn Care** – Watering plants, pulling weeds, or raking leaves.

Real-Life Example: Meet Emily!

Emily, an 8-year-old entrepreneur, started her own **lemonade stand**. She added unique flavors like **strawberry and mint** to make her drinks stand out. Soon, customers lined up, and she saved enough money to buy a new bike!

What You Can Learn from Emily:

- **Be creative!** Think of ways to make your business unique.

- **Market yourself!** Tell friends, family, and neighbors about your business.

- **Save a portion of your earnings** for future investments!

3.1.5 Creative Crafts: Selling Handmade Goods

Do you love making things with your hands? If so, you already have the skills to start a **handmade craft business!** Handcrafted items are special because they are **one-of-a-kind and made with care.**

Why Do People Love Handmade Goods?

People love buying **personal and unique** things. A store might sell the same bracelet to thousands of people, but **a bracelet made by you is one of a kind!**

Here's how to **turn your creativity into cash:**

1. **Choose what to make** – Friendship bracelets, keychains, stickers, or painted mugs!

2. **Make a few samples** – Show them to family and friends for feedback.

3. **Set up a selling space** – Use a local fair, school event, or online store!

4. **Price your work** – Make sure your prices cover the cost of materials **plus** a little extra for profit.

Example: The Power of Personalization

Emily made handmade notebooks, but they didn't sell well. Then, she added customers' names on the covers, and suddenly everyone wanted one! **Adding personal touches makes items more special!**

Try It: What do **you love making** that others might want to buy?

 ## 3.1.6 Recycling for Bucks: The Eco-Friendly Way to Earn

Did you know that your **trash could be turned into cash**? Many recycling centers **pay money** for certain materials, such as aluminum cans and plastic bottles. This is a great way to earn extra money and help **the planet!**

How to Start a Recycling Business

1. **Find out what recyclables are worth money** in your area (like cans, glass bottles, or paper).

2. **Ask family and neighbors if they have recyclables** they don't need.

3. **Set up collection bins** at home and sort items to

make them easy to drop off.

4. **Visit a recycling center** to exchange your materials for cash!

Recycling is great because:

- It **reduces waste** in the environment.
- It **teaches responsibility** and work ethic.
- It **turns small efforts into big savings!**

Challenge Yourself: Can you collect 100 bottles in one month? Then, see how much money you can earn!

 ## 3.1.7 Key Takeaways

✔ **Earning money isn't just about chores—it's about creativity and responsibility!**

✔ **Entrepreneurship helps kids turn hobbies into cash!**

✔ **Planning and tracking earnings leads to smarter financial decisions!**

✔ **The more effort and creativity you put in, the more you can earn!**

 ## 3.1.8 Glossary

- **Entrepreneur** – Someone who starts their own business to earn money.

- **Chore Contract** – An agreement on what chores to do and how much they pay.

- **Investment** – Spending money on something that will help you earn more later.

- **Profit** – The money left after paying for materials and supplies.

- **Marketing** – Telling others about your product or service so they want to buy it.

Final Thoughts

Earning money can be **fun, creative, and rewarding!** Whether it's **starting a small business, selling crafts, or helping out at home**, the skills you learn today will help you become **a smart and independent earner!**

What's your next earning adventure? Plan it, try it, and start making money today!

3.2 The Art of Saving

Why Saving is More Than Just a Piggy Bank

Saving money is like planting a tree. The more you take care of it, the bigger it grows! But saving isn't just about stuffing coins into a piggy bank—it's about making smart choices that help your money **grow over time**. Let's explore different ways to save and how to **make your money work for you!**

 ### 3.2.1 Learning Objectives

By the end of this section, you will:

- Understand different ways to save money.
- Learn how a savings account works.
- Discover how interest helps money grow.
- Set savings goals and track progress.

3.2.2 Beyond the Piggy Bank

Meet **Jamie**, a young saver from Pennsville. Jamie loved collecting coins in a piggy bank. Still, one day, Uncle Mike shared a secret about a **magical place** where money **grows on its own**—a savings account! Intrigued, Jamie decided to open one and learn more about how money can **work smarter, not harder.**

Jamie's adventure begins at the bank, where a friendly **Banker Guide** explains that a savings account is like a treasure chest for money. Not only is it **safe**, but it also earns something special—**Interest**. Interest is like a reward from a bank for keeping your money with them. It's like planting and watching a tiny seed **sprout more coins over time!**

Why Open a Savings Account?

- **Safe Storage** – Money in a bank is safer than cash at home.
- **Earn Interest** – Your money grows over time without you doing extra work.
- **Set Goals** – Helps you plan for big purchases like a bike or a game console.

Jamie learned how to **set goals** using a progress tracking chart. By depositing money regularly, Jamie saw savings grow and felt a sense of **achievement** and **independence**.

 3.2.3 My First Bank Visit: A Practical Guide

Imagine stepping into a bank with your parents. The doors swing open, and you hear the chatter of customers, the beep of ATMs, and the clink-clank of coins in a counting machine. **This is where money magic happens!**

Why Visit the Bank with a Parent?

Opening a bank account is a **big step**, and having a parent or guardian there helps! They can **explain things**, help with **paperwork**, and ask important **questions**. Plus, you'll feel more confident knowing someone you trust is there to guide you.

Meet Alex: A First-Time Bank Visitor

Alex was **excited and nervous** about opening a savings account. A friendly **bank teller** greeted Alex and explained how the bank works.

Alex learned:

- **A deposit** means putting money into the account (feeding your savings!).
- **A withdrawal** means taking money out when needed.
- **Online banking** lets you check your savings from anywhere!

How to Prepare for Your First Bank Visit

- **Bring money** – You'll need some to open your account.
- **Take identification** – A birth certificate or passport is required.
- **Prepare questions** – Ask, "What is interest?" or "How can I track my savings?"

Role-Playing Activity

Try practicing your bank visit at home with a family member! One person can be the **customer**, and the other plays the **bank teller**.

Practice saying:

"Hi, I'd like to open a savings account." and "How does interest help my money grow?"

This way, you'll feel **ready and confident** when your bank visit arrives!

3.2.4 The Magic of Interest on Savings: Watch Your Money Grow

Imagine your savings as a **magical beanstalk**. Every dollar you save is like planting a **magic bean**. Over time, these beans don't just sit there—they **sprout into more dollars**! This happens because of **Interest**, the extra money banks **give you as a thank-you** for saving.

Simple vs. Compound Interest

Simple Interest

This is when the bank pays you extra money, or Interest, **only on the original amount you saved**.

Compound Interest

Money grows **on what you save + the Interest you already earned**! This means your savings grow **faster and bigger** over time.

Example

Let's imagine **two friends, Jake and Mia**, both decide to save **$1,000** in a savings account.

- **Jake's account earns Simple Interest** – He earns **5% interest per year only on the original $1,000**.

- **Mia's account earns Compound Interest** – She earns 5% interest per year, which applies to her growing balance!

Let's see how their money grows over **3 years:**

Year	Jake (Simple Interest: 5% per year)	Mia (Compound Interest: 5% per year)
1	$1,000 + $50 = $1,050	$1,000 + $50 = $1,050
2	$1,050 + $50 = $1,100	$1,050 + $52.50 = $1,102.50
3	$1,100 + $50 = $1,150	$1,102.50 + $55.13 = $1,157.63

At the end of **3 years**:

- **Jake's account with Simple Interest = $1,150**

- **Mia's account with Compound Interest = $1,157.63**

Mia made **$7.63 more** than Jake – **without adding any extra money!**

Now imagine if **they saved for 10 or 20 years**—Mia's account would grow **much faster** than Jake's because **her interest earns more each year!**

Why Does This Matter?

✔ The earlier you start saving, the more your money **grows over time**.

✔ Compound interest works best when you **save money and leave it alone!** ✔ **Even small savings today** can turn into **big savings in the future**!

Challenge: Try calculating how much **$1,000 would grow in 10 years** with **simple vs. compound Interest**! You'll see just how powerful **compounding really is!**

Challenge: Try calculating how much **$1,000 would grow in 10 years** with **simple vs. compound interest**! You'll see just how powerful **compounding really is!**

3.2.5 The Magic of Starting Early: Why Time is Your Best Friend

Now that you've seen the **power of compound interest,** you might be wondering:

- How do I make the most of it?
- When should I start saving?
- How often should I save?

The answer is **simple—the earlier you start and the more regularly you save, the more your money will grow!**

Saving money **isn't just about how much you save—it's about how long your money has time to grow!**

Lest have a look and Jake and Mia.

- **Mia starts saving early at age 10.** She saves **$10 per month** in an account that earns **5% compound interest per year**.

- **Jake waits until he's 16 to start saving.** He also saves **$10 per month** at the same interest rate.

By the time they **both turn 20**, let's see how their savings compare.

Age	Mia (Started Saving at 10)	Jake (Started Saving at 16)
10	$10	$0
11	$123	$0
12	$253	$0
13	$392	$0
14	$540	$0
15	$698	$0
16	$867	$10
17	$1,048	$123
18	$1,243	$253
19	$1,453	$392
20	$1,679	$540

What Happened?

Even though **Mia and Jake saved the exact same amount per month**...

- **Mia ended up with more than 3x the amount of Jake**—just because she started earlier!

- **Why?** Because **Mia's money had more time to grow with compound interest!**

3.2.6 The Catch-Up Problem: Why Waiting to Save is a Mistake

Jake realizes **he's far behind Mia** and wants to **catch up.**

But here's the problem: **The longer you wait to start saving, the harder it is to catch up!**

To have the **same amount as Mia by age 20,** Jake would have to:

- **Save 3X more per month** (instead of just $10, he'd have to save $30)

- **Hope for a higher interest rate** (which isn't always possible)

- **Keep saving for many more years than Mia did**

This is why **starting early is so important**—time does a lot of the work for you!

3.2.7 Why Saving Regularly is Just as Important

Starting early is great, but **saving regularly** makes the biggest difference. Think of it like **watering a plant**—if you water it once and forget about it, it won't grow much. But if you **water it a little every week**, it will grow tall and strong!

Example: The Snowball Effect

If you save just **$1 every day**, you'll have:

- **$30 in one month**
- **$365 in one year**
- **$3,650 in ten years!**

3.2.8 Smart Saver Action Plan

Want to be **like Mia** and get ahead with saving? Follow these steps:

- **Step 1: Start saving NOW—even if it's just a tiny amount!**
- **Step 2: Set a regular habit—can you save $1 a day or $5 a week?**
- **Step 3: Watch your savings grow!** Keep track of your progress with a **Savings Tracker**.

IMPORTANT

✔ Start saving as early as possible—even small amounts grow over time.
✔ The longer your money has to grow, the more powerful compound Interest becomes!
✔ Don't wait to save—your future self will thank you! Like Mia, start saving today and let time do the work for you!

 ## 3.2.9 Key Takeaways

✔ Saving money helps prepare for the future.

✔ A savings account is a safe place where money grows over time.

✔ Interest is extra money banks give you for saving.

✔ Setting savings goals makes it easier to reach big dreams!

 ## 3.2.10 Glossary

- **Savings Account** – A special bank account that keeps money safe and earns interest.
- **Deposit** – Putting money into a savings account.
- **Withdrawal** – Taking money out when needed.
- **Interest** – Extra money the bank pays you for keeping savings with them.
- **Compound Interest** – Interest that builds on itself, helping money grow even faster!

Final Thoughts

Saving money is **a superpower!** Whether saving for a **new toy, a big adventure, or your future**, every coin you save **brings you one step closer to your goals**.

3.3 Budgeting Basics for Beginners

Why Budgeting is a Superpower!

Imagine trying to build the best fort, but you run out of pillows and blankets halfway through. If you had planned ahead, you could have ensured you had **enough materials to finish! That's what Budgeting does for your money**—it helps you **plan** to get what you want **without running out too soon.**

Budgeting is like a **treasure map** for your money. It helps you **decide where your money should go** so you don't accidentally spend it all on snacks when you want to buy a new game! Let's learn how to **take control of your money** and use it wisely.

3.3.1 Learning Objectives

By the end of this section, you will:

- **Understand what budgeting is and why it's important.**
- **Learn how to create a budget step by step.**
- **Use fun activities to track spending and savings.**
- **Make smart decisions about money for fun and important purchases.**

3.3.2 What is Budgeting?

A budget is **a plan for your money**—it helps you **decide how much to save, spend, and share**. When you budget, you make sure you have money for the things you **need** while still being able to afford things you **want**.

Why is Budgeting Important?

- **Prevents overspending** – You won't run out of money too quickly.
- **Helps reach goals** – You can save for bigger things like a bike or a trip.
- **Teaches responsibility** – Learning how to manage money now will help you in the future!

3.3.3 Why It's Important to Track Income and Expenses Before Making a Budget

Before creating **a budget**, you must **understand where your money is coming from and where it's going**. That's why **tracking income and expenses** is the **first step** to managing money wisely. Because you can't plan where your money should go if you don't know **how much you have** or **how much you're spending**

Imagine filling a jar with water **without knowing how big the jar is** – you might **run out of water too soon** or **spill too much**. That happens when you don't track money—you might **spend too much too quickly** or **not save enough** for what you want. **That's exactly why you need to budget!**

Why is Tracking Your Money Important?

Helps You See Where Your Money is Going

- Without tracking, you might **accidentally spend too much** on small things (like snacks or toys).
    - **Example:** If you realize you're spending **$10 a week on snacks**, you might decide to **cut back and save that money for something bigger!**

Helps You Understand Your Spending Habits

- Are you spending more than you earn?
- Are you **saving enough** for your goals?
- Tracking **shows you patterns** so you can **make better choices**.

Helps You Set Realistic Budget Goals

- How can you set a budget if you don't know how much money you **earn and spend**?
    - **Example:** If you get **a $20 allowance** but spend **$15 right away**, you only have **$5 left**—knowing this **helps you plan better next time**.

Stops You From Running Out of Money Too Soon

- Have you ever spent all your money **too quickly** and then couldn't buy something important?
- Tracking your money helps you **make smarter spending decisions**.

Prevents "Where Did My Money Go?!" Moments

- You'll **never wonder where your money disappeared** if you track your spending.
- You can **look back** and see exactly what you spent on!

 ### 3.3.4 Activity – Track Your Income & Expenses Like a Pro!

A **Money Tracker Sheet** helps kids (and adults!) **keep track of where their money is going.** It's like a **diary for your money,** showing how much you **earn, spend,** and **save** every day.

How to Use a Money Tracker Sheet

Step 1: Track Your Money

- **Income:** Write down any money received (allowance, gifts, chore earnings).
- **Expenses:** List everything you spend money on (toys, snacks, savings, giving).
- **Balance:** Calculate what's left!

Step 2: Add Up Your Totals

- **How much did you spend?**
- **How much did you save?**
- **What's left? (Balance)**

Step 3: Reflect on Your Spending

- **Did you spend more than you planned?**
- **Did you save enough for your goal?**
- **What would you change next time?**

3.3.5 Balancing Spending and Saving: The Best of Both Worlds!

Sometimes, when you get money, you might feel like you have to **choose** between spending **or** saving—but guess what? **You can do both!** Instead of spending everything immediately or saving every penny, you can **split your money** into different parts. This way, you get to enjoy a little now while still working towards something bigger in the future.

Smart money management isn't about never spending – it's about **finding the right balance between spending and saving.**

Why balancing is important:

- If you **spend everything right away**, you might not have enough for something big later.

- If you **save everything** without Budgeting for fun, you might feel frustrated and tempted to overspend later.

- A good balance helps you **enjoy your money and plan for bigger goals!**

The "Spend Some, Save Some" Approach

Let's say you get **$20** from allowance, a birthday gift, or for helping around the house. Instead of spending it all at once, try this method:

- **Spend 50%** on something fun today (**$10**)

- **Save 40%** for a bigger goal (**$8**)

- **Give 10%** to help others or invest for the future (**$2**)

Why is this a great idea?

- You get to enjoy your money **without feeling guilty**

about spending.

- You still **save for something bigger** that will make you happy later.

- You learn **how to manage money wisely**, just like adults do!

How "Spend a Little, Save the Rest" Works in Real Life

Example 1: Buying a Toy While Saving for a Bike

Leo wants a bike ($100) but sees a cool **action figure ($10)** at the store. If Leo spends all his money on small toys, he'll never reach his bike goal. Instead, he **buys one action figure today ($10) and saves the other $10 toward his bike goal.**

Outcome: Leo enjoys something **right away** while progressing toward his bigger dream!

Example 2: The Ice Cream vs. Concert Choice

Ella gets **a $15 allowance each week**. She really wants to **see her favorite singer in concert ($60 ticket)** but also **loves ice cream ($5 each week). If she spends $5 on ice cream and saves $10 each week in six weeks, she'll have enough for the concert!**

Outcome: Ella **enjoys small weekly treats** but still reaches her big savings goal on time!

3.3.6 Activity – How to Create Your Own Budget

Once you understand **how much money you earn and spend,** you can **build a simple budget.**

Step 1: Write Down Your Income

This is the money you **receive**—allowance, gifts, money from chores, or even small business earnings. Knowing how much money you have helps you plan wisely!

Step 2: List Your Expenses

Expenses are things you spend money on. Split them into two groups:

- **Needs** – Things you must have (food, school supplies, saving for big goals).
- **Wants** – Fun things you'd like (toys, snacks, entertainment).

Step 3: Decide How Much to Save, Spend & Share

A simple way to budget is using the **50/30/20 Rule:**

- **50% for Needs & Goals** – Important things and savings.
- **30% for Wants** – Fun stuff like treats and toys.
- **20% for Giving or Investing** – Helping others or saving for future opportunities.

- **Example:** If you get **$20 per week**
    - Save $8, Spend $6, Keep $4 for a big goal!

Step 4: Track Your Spending

Use a **Money Tracker** to write down your spending each day. This will help you see if you're following your budget and what you need to adjust!

3.3.7 Key Takeaways

✔ **A budget is a plan that helps you manage money wisely.**

✔ **Budgeting helps prevent overspending and reach goals.**

✔ **Tracking your spending lets you see where your money goes.**

✔ Understand you can s**pend and save at the same time** (fun now and rewards later.)

✔ **Smart choices lead to more fun and less stress about money!**

3.4.8 Glossary

- **Budget** – A plan for how to use money wisely.
- **Income** – Money you receive (allowance, gifts, earnings).

- **Expenses** – Things you spend money on (needs & wants).

- **Savings** – Money set aside for future goals.

- **Money Tracker** – A tool to record spending and saving.

Final Thoughts

Budgeting is a **superpower** that helps you **control your money** instead of wondering where it went. Whether saving for a **fun trip, a cool new toy, or something important**, a budget **makes it possible!**

What's your next money goal? Start your budget today and make it happen!

3.4 Digital Safety in Spending: Smart Choices Online

Welcome to the World of Digital Money!

Welcome to the world of **digital money!** Today, you can buy your favorite toy or snack without using cash. But with great power comes great responsibility—let's learn how to **stay safe online!**

 **3.4.1 Learning Objectives**

By the end of this section, you will:

- Understand what digital money is and how it works.
- Learn about different types of digital transactions.
- Recognize the benefits and risks of digital money.

- **Develop safe online spending habits.**

3.4.2 Understanding Online Money

Think of yourself as a **young digital money wizard** who can pay for things with just a tap or click. Instead of using cash, digital money lets you **buy items online, use debit and credit cards, and store cash in e-wallets on your phone.**

Different Types of Digital Money:

- **Debit Cards** – Take money **directly** from your bank account when you buy something.

- **Credit Cards** – Borrow money from the bank and pay it back later. **(Adults ONLY)**

- **E-Wallets & Apps** – Apps like Apple Pay, Google Pay, or PayPal hold your money digitally.

- **Online Transactions** – Buy things from websites instead of going to a store.

Why Is Digital Money So Amazing?

- **Super Convenient** – No more digging through your pockets for coins!

- **Fast Transactions** – Tap, swipe, or click to complete your purchase.

- **Shop from Anywhere** – Buy things online without leaving home.

However, **digital money also has risks**. Imagine someone sneaking into your piggy bank and taking your coins! That's why keeping your digital money **safe and secure is crucial**.

3.4.3 The Pros & Cons of Digital Money

Like everything, digital money has its **advantages and disadvantages**. Let's compare!

Pros:

✔ **Easy to Use** – Tap, swipe, or click!

✔ **Fast Transactions** – No need to wait for change.

✔ **Track Spending** – Digital records help you see where your money goes.

✔ **Buy Online** – You can shop from anywhere in the world!

Cons:

X **Easy to Overspend** – Since you don't see physical cash, spending too much is easy.

X **Security Risks** – If not protected, hackers could steal personal information.

X **Technical Issues** – If the internet is down, you might be unable to pay.

Smart Tip – Always check your balance and spending habits to ensure you're not using too much digital money!

3.4.4 Staying Safe with Digital Money

Using digital money is **easy and fun**, but being responsible and protecting your personal information is essential.

How to Keep Your Digital Money Safe:

- **Use Strong Passwords** – Create unique passwords like P@ssw0rd123 and never share them.

- **Never Share Personal Information or Passwords** – Never give your bank details pr passwords to strangers.

- **Use only trusted websites and apps** – Look for the **lock symbol ()** in the address bar when shopping online.

- **Turn on Notifications** – Many banks send alerts when money is spent, so you always know what's happening.

The Safe Online Checklist

Before clicking "buy" on a website, ask yourself:

- **Is this website safe?** (Look for the lock symbol!)

- **Am I using a secure internet connection?**

- **Do I really need this item?**

- **Ask a parent or adult before making online purchases.**

3.4.5 Digital Money in the Future

The world of money is changing! Some countries are already **going cashless**, meaning they only use digital payments. New types of digital money, like **cryptocurrencies (Bitcoin, Ethereum, etc.),** are also becoming popular.

What Could the Future Look Like?

- **More cashless stores** – Some shops may stop accepting physical money!

- **AI and banking apps** – Smart apps may help you manage your money better.

- **New ways to earn and save** – Digital investments and automated savings may become common.

Even though technology is changing, **the most important thing is to be smart with your money!** Whether using cash or digital dollars, **being responsible and thinking before spending is always a great habit.**

 ## 3.4.6 Key Takeaways

✔ **Digital money lets you pay online and use e-wallets, debit cards, and credit cards.**

✔ **It's fast and easy to use, but you must keep your information secure.**

✔ **Always check websites, use strong passwords, and track your spending!**

✔ **Digital money is the future, but smart money habits always stay the same!**

 ## 3.4.7 Glossary

- **Digital Money** – Money stored electronically instead of as cash.

- **E-Wallet** – A digital tool (like PayPal or Apple Pay) that holds money.

- **Online Transactions** – Buying things on the internet using digital payments.

- **Cybersecurity** – Protecting your digital money and personal data from hackers.

Final Thoughts

Digital money is like having a **superpower**—you can pay for things with a tap, swipe, or click! But with great power comes great responsibility. **Always be careful, spend wisely, and protect your money!**

What's your next digital purchase? Think before you spend, and make smart money moves!

> ## Keep Going!
>
> If something doesn't make sense right away, that's okay! You can:
> - **Review a section**
> - **Ask a parent or teacher for help**
> - **Try a hands-on activity**
>
> Every step you take brings you closer to being a money-smart pro! **Keep learning, exploring, and having fun with money!**

Transition to Module 4: Smart Spending

Great job! You've learned how to **earn money** and make a plan to **save it wisely**—but what happens when it's time to **spend**?

Not all spending is the same. Some purchases help you reach your goals, while others can quickly drain your savings if you're not careful. In **Module 4: Smart Spending**, we'll explore:

How to make wise spending choices
The difference between needs and wants
How to compare prices and get the best deals
Why planning your spending helps you avoid regrets

Get ready to become a **smart spender** who knows how to make every dollar count!

Help Others by Sharing Your Review!

Your Words Can Make a Big Difference!

"The more you give, the more you have. That's the magic of kindness!" – Unknown

Just like saving money helps us reach our goals, sharing what we've learned helps others find their way too!

Would you help another family start their financial adventure?

Many parents and kids are looking for fun, easy ways to learn about money—but they're not sure where to start. That's where **YOU** come in!

Your review can help someone decide if this book is right for their family. It's like leaving a helpful signpost on a trail—guiding others in the right direction. And the best part? It's completely free and only takes a minute!

Why Your Review Matters

When you leave a review, you can help:

✔ One more kid feel confident about money

✔ One more family have fun learning together

✔ One more child start a savings goal

✔ One more dream become a reality!

How to Leave a Review

It's easy! Just scan the QR code below or visit this link: https://www.amazon.com/review/review-your-purchases/?asin=BOOKASIN

Write a few sentences about what you liked—maybe your favorite lesson or activity!

Did your child enjoy designing their own money?
Did they set a savings goal for something exciting?
Did the book make learning about money fun?

Every review helps. And if you love helping others, you're exactly the kind of person who makes a difference!

Thank you from the bottom of my heart!

— **Rachael Miller**

MODULE 4
SMART SPENDING – MAKING WISE MONEY CHOICES

4.1 Taking Saving to the Next Level

Smart Saving Strategies

Saving Money isn't just about putting coins in a jar—it's about **creating smart habits** that help you prepare for the future. Whether saving for something **fun**, planning for an **unexpected expense**, or investing in **your future self**, learning to **save wisely** will help you become **financially independent and stress-free**.

In this section, we'll explore **advanced saving strategies** that will help you **stay in control of your Money and build a strong financial foundation**.

 ### 4.1.1 Learning Objectives

What You'll Learn in This Module:

- Learn **how to create an advanced savings plan**.
- Understand **why emergency savings are essential**.

- Discover **how time and effort affect money choices**.

- See how **small sacrifices today can lead to bigger rewards later**.

- Learn how to **use savings apps and tools to grow your Money**.

4.1.2 The Power of Smart Saving: Why It's More Than Just Stashing Money

Think of **saving Money as something like building a house. If** you plan and make it carefully, it will **protect you and provide opportunities for the future.**

Why Saving Smart Matters:

✔ **Protects you from surprises** – No more worrying about sudden expenses.

✔ **Helps you reach big goals faster** – A new bike? A trip? Saving helps you get there!

✔ **Teaches financial independence** – The better you manage your savings, the more control you have over your Money.

4.1.3 Emergency Savings – Why It's Smart to Save for Unexpected Things

Smart savers don't just save for fun things. They also save for **unexpected situations**, like if their bike gets a flat tire or they need extra Money for a school project. Having an

emergency fund means you won't have to borrow Money when surprises happen!

What is an emergency savings fund?

It's **Money set aside for surprises**—things you don't expect but need to handle quickly, like:

- A broken bike that needs fixing
- School supplies you lost and need to replace

Why is an Emergency Emergency Fund Important?

✔ **Prepares you for surprises** – Life doesn't always go as planned!

✔ **Reduces stress** – You'll feel calm and in control if you know you have Money saved.

✔ **Keeps you from borrowing** – You won't have to ask for Money last minute.

How to Build an Emergency Fund

1. **Start a "Rainy Day Jar"** or a separate bank account called an "Emergency Fund" – a special savings account for surprises.
2. **Set a Small Weekly Goal** – Save $1–$5 weekly.
3. **Think of Possible Emergencies**—Write down things you might need to save for (e.g., a broken bike, a lost book, a school trip).

4.1.4 Understanding the Value of Time and Money

Money isn't just about what you have—it's also about how much time and effort it takes to earn it.

Think About This:

- **If you earn $5 for lawn mowing, a new toy costs $25...**
- **That means you need to mow 5 lawns to afford it.**

Would you still want to buy it if you had to mow 5 lawns for it?

Why This is Important

- Teaches you to **think before spending**
- Helps you decide if a purchase is **really worth it**
- Encourages you to **spend Money on things that truly matter**

4.1.5 Using Savings Apps and Tools

Technology makes saving **easier than ever**! Some savings apps can **automate your savings**, while others help you **track your goals**.

Types of Savings Apps & Tools

- **Automatic Savings Apps** – Move Money into savings without you thinking about it!

- **Examples:** Acorns, Qapital

- **Budgeting & Goal-Tracking Apps** – Help you see where your Money goes.

  - **Examples:** YNAB (You Need a Budget), Greenlight

- **Savings Gamification Apps** – Turn saving into a fun game!

  - **Examples:** PiggyBot, Bankaroo

- **Banking & Investment Apps** – Help kids learn about managing and growing Money.

  - **Examples:** GoHenry, Stash

How to Use These Tools in Your Savings Plan

- **Pick an app that matches your needs** (Do you want automatic savings? Budget tracking? A fun game?)
- **Set a savings goal and track your progress**
- **Automate savings whenever possible**

The right tools make saving Money easier and more fun!

 ## 4.1.6 Key Takeaways

✔ **Emergency savings help you handle unexpected expenses without stress.**

✔ **Money isn't just about spending—it's also about the time and effort it takes to earn it.**

✔ **Using savings tools and apps makes saving easier and more fun!**

✔ **The best savers turn small habits into BIG success!**

 ## 4.1.7 Glossary

- **Advanced Savings** – A strategy where you save money in different ways, like using a savings account, investing, or setting up long-term savings goals.

- **Emergency Fund** – Money set aside for unexpected expenses, like fixing a broken toy or replacing a lost item.

- **Budgeting Methods** – Different ways to organize your money, such as the "50-30-20 rule" (saving 50%, spending 30%, and using 20% for extra expenses).

- **Spending Plan** – A plan that helps you decide where your money should go so you don't run out too soon.

- **Impulse Buying** – When you buy something without planning or thinking about it first.

- **Short-Term vs. Long-Term Savings** – Short-term savings are for things you want soon (like a toy), while long-term savings help you reach bigger goals (like a bike or a trip).

- **Interest** – Extra money that banks or investments give you for keeping your money with them.

- **Financial Responsibility** – Making smart choices with your money, like not spending everything at once and saving for the future.

- **Smart Spending** – Thinking before you buy to make sure you're making a good choice.

Final Thoughts

Take Charge of Your Savings Today!

By now, you've learned that **saving Money is more than just stashing coins in a piggy bank**—it's about **building smart habits that will set you up for a strong financial future**.

Money is a tool; when you **learn how to use it wisely**, you **gain power over your financial future**. Whether saving for something fun, preparing for an emergency, or learning to make thoughtful money choices, you are now equipped with strategies to **help you make your savings work for you**.

4.2 Advanced Budgeting Methods

Take Your Budgeting to the Next Level!

Once you've mastered the basics of Budgeting, it's time to **level up!** Advanced budgeting techniques can help you **manage money smarter, plan for the Future, and grow your savings over time.**

In this section, you'll learn **about different types of budgets, how to plan for long-term goals, and why Budgeting can sometimes feel hard—but it is totally worth it!**

 ### 4.2.1 Learning Objectives

What You'll Learn in This Module:

- **Plan for future expenses** so you're never caught off guard.
- **Learn how to budget** for fun spending without

running out of money.

- **Understand opportunity cost**—choosing between two things you really want.
- **Adjust a budget** when unexpected expenses come up.
- **Explore different budgeting styles** and find what works for you.

4.2.2 Different Types of Budgets: Find the Best Fit for You!

Not everyone **budgets the same way**. Some people like to **track every dollar**, while others prefer a **more flexible approach**. Here are three advanced budgeting methods—**try them out and see which works best for you!**

Zero-Based Budgeting – Every Dollar Has a Job

This method **assigns every dollar you receive to a specific purpose**—spending, saving, or giving. At the end of the month, your **budget should equal zero** because every dollar has been planned for!

Example:

- If you earn **$100 this month**, you could divide it like this:
    - **$50 for savings**
    - **$30 for fun**

- **$20 for giving**

- At the end of the month, **you don't have "extra" money sitting around**—you have a plan for it!

Zero-based Budgeting **helps prevent wasteful spending** because every dollar has a **specific purpose**!

The Envelope System – A Cash-Based Budgeting Trick

This method helps you **stay on track by physically setting aside money** for different categories. It works for both **actual cash envelopes and digital budgeting apps**.

How It Works:

- Label different envelopes with **food, fun, savings, and giving** categories.

- Put your money into each envelope at the start of the month.

- **Once an envelope is empty, you can't spend more in that category!**

The envelope system **teaches self-discipline** because once the money is gone, it's gone!

Percentage-Based Budgeting – Customize Your Budget!

Instead of assigning **specific dollar amounts**, this method uses **percentages** so your budget adjusts when your income changes.

Example:

Instead of using the common **50/30/20 rule** (50% needs, 30% wants, 20% savings), you might customize it to:

- **40% savings** (big goal-focused!)
- **40% needs** (essentials)
- **20% fun** (treat yourself responsibly!)

This system is great because it **automatically adjusts when your income changes**!

4.2.3 Budgeting for Long-Term Goals: Planning for the Future!

Budgeting isn't just about **what you want now**—it's also about **preparing for things in the Future**. Long-term Budgeting helps you **break big goals into smaller steps**, making them easier to reach!

Short-Term Goals (1-6 months)

- Saving for a **bike, video game, or a fun experience** like an amusement park trip.

These goals are **quick wins**—you'll see your progress fast!

Medium-Term Goals (6 months-3 years)

- Saving for **school supplies, a hobby, or a bigger trip**.

Requires **consistent saving** and **sticking to your budget!**

Long-Term Goals (3+ years)

- Thinking ahead for **a car, going to college, or even moving out one day**.

These take **patience**, but **starting early makes them easier**!

The earlier you **start saving for long-term goals**, the easier they are to achieve!

> **Tip – Break big goals into smaller steps! Instead of saying, "I need $500," say, "I'll save $10 a week for a year."**

4.2.4 The Emotional Side of Budgeting: Why It Feels Hard Sometimes

Let's be honest—Budgeting **isn't always easy**. Sometimes, you **see something cool in a store and want to spend your money right away**. Other times, it **feels like saving is taking forever**.

Here's why Budgeting can feel tough—and how to **stay on track**!

Delayed Gratification vs. Impulse Spending

It can be **tempting to spend money immediately**, especially when you see something exciting. But **waiting to buy something bigger later** often **feels better** than spending all your money now on something small.

Example:

- **Impulse Spending:** Buying **a $5 snack every day**—but not saving for something big.

- **Delayed Gratification:** Waiting **2 months** to buy a **$100 new game**—and feeling **so much prouder** when you can afford it!

Lesson: Learning to **wait before spending** helps you make **better choices and reach bigger goals**!

The Money Mindset Shift: Budgeting = More Fun, Not Less!

Some people think **Budgeting means no fun**, but **it means MORE fun in the Future**!

Example:

- Without a budget, → You spend money randomly and can't afford big things.

- With a budget → You **plan ahead**, so you always have enough for the **best experiences!**

Lesson: A budget **isn't about stopping fun**—it's about making sure you can afford even better things!

 ## 4.2.5 Activity – Test Your Budgeting & Saving Skills!

Challenge 1: Budget for Two Months Using Different Methods!

- **Month 1:** Try **Zero-Based Budgeting** (assign every dollar a job).
- **Month 2:** Try **Percentage-Based Budgeting** (ex: 40% savings, 40% needs, 20% fun).
- **Compare:** Which one works best for you?

Challenge 2: Plan a Long-Term Budget for a Big Goal!

- Pick **something big** (a new bike, a gaming console, or a trip).
- **Break it down**—how much do you need to save each month?
- **Stick to your plan!**

Challenge 3: Calculate Compound Interest on $1,000 for 10 Years!

- Use an online **compound interest calculator** to see how much $1,000 would grow in 10 years!

 ## 4.2.6 Key Takeaways

✔ **Different budgeting methods work for different people**—try **Zero-Based, Envelope, or Percentage-Based Budgeting** to see what fits your style!

✔ **Budgeting isn't just about today—it's about planning for the Future!** Learn to **budget for short-term,**

medium-term, and long-term goals, so you're always prepared.

✔ **Fun spending needs a budget too!** Setting a **limit on fun spending** helps you enjoy money **without running out too soon**.

✔ **Opportunity cost matters!** Every time you spend on **one thing, you give up another**—choose wisely.

✔ **Budgets must be flexible!** If something unexpected happens, **adjust your budget instead of giving up**.

✔ **Saving early helps your money grow!** The **longer you save and invest, the more you'll have in the Future**.

✔ **Budgeting doesn't stop fun—it creates more fun!** Planning ahead **helps you afford even bigger experiences and opportunities**!

 ## 4.2.7 Glossary

- **Zero-Based Budgeting** – A budgeting method where **every dollar you receive is assigned a job** — nothing is left unplanned!

- **Envelope System** – A budgeting system where you **set aside cash (or digital amounts) for different categories** like food, fun, and savings. Once an envelope is empty, you **can't spend more in that category!**

- **Percentage-Based Budgeting** – A budgeting system where **you assign a percentage of your money** to different categories (example: **40% savings, 40%**

needs, 20% fun!**).

- **Long-Term Budgeting** – Planning your money **for future goals** like a **bike, a trip, or even college** instead of just focusing on today.

- **Flexible Budgeting** – A budgeting method where **you adjust your plan when unexpected things happen** (for example, If you planned $15 for snacks but only spent $10, you move the extra $5 to savings!).

- **Opportunity Cost** – The **thing you give up** when you spend money on something else (for example, If you buy a toy today, you might have to **wait longer for a bigger goal!**).

- **Delayed Gratification** – Waiting to buy something **so you can afford something even better later**—one of the most important money skills!

- **Financial Discipline** – Learning to **control spending, plan ahead, and make smart money decisions** instead of spending everything right away.

Final Thoughts

Budgeting = Freedom!

A **budget doesn't limit you**—it **gives you power** over your money to reach bigger goals, prepare for surprises, and **always have enough for what matters most!**

What's your next step? Try an advanced budgeting method this month and take control of your finances!

4.3 Empowering Financial Independence

Becoming the Boss of Your Money

Taking control of your money isn't just about saving and spending—it's about **understanding how to make smart financial choices, learning from mistakes, and planning for the future**. Financial independence doesn't mean having unlimited money—it means having the **freedom to make choices that support your goals, dreams, and lifestyle**, and the resilience and growth that come from learning from financial mistakes.

In this section, we'll explore **decision-making strategies, learning from financial mistakes, and creating a financial freedom plan to take charge of your money and future.**

 4.3.1 Learning Objectives

What You'll Learn in This Module:

- Making smart spending choices.
- **Develop smart decision-making strategies for handling money.**
- **Understand why financial independence is about taking responsibility for your money.**

4.3.2 Reflection Section: Decision-Making Strategies

Every money decision you make has an impact. Whether **saving for a goal, spending on something fun, or planning ahead,** learning **to make smart choices** is key to **financial independence.**

The "Think Before You Spend" Strategy

Every time you spend money, you decide—but is it always the best? Sometimes, we **buy things on impulse** (without thinking), only to **regret it later.** Learning how to **pause and think** before spending can help you make **smarter financial choices** and ensure you **get the most value for your money.**

Before you buy something, ask yourself:

- **Do I really need this or want it right now?**
    - Is this something that **will be useful for a long time,** or is it just exciting at the moment?
- **Can I get it for a lower price somewhere else?**
    - Is there a **sale, discount, or second-hand option** that would let me save money?
- **Will I still want this next week?**
    - Sometimes, we want something **a lot** at first, but the excitement fades quickly.
- **Will this purchase bring me long-term happiness or just short-term excitement?**
    - Will **I still be using or enjoying this item a month from now?**
- **What else could I do with this money?**
    - If I don't buy this, could I use the money for **something more important or exciting later**?

4.3.3 The "24-Hour Wait Rule": A Simple Trick to Avoid Buying Things You Don't Need

Have you ever bought something only to regret it later?

One of the best ways to avoid **impulse purchases** is to **wait before buying**.

Here's how the "24-Hour Wait Rule" works:

1. **If you see something you want to buy, WAIT 24 HOURS before purchasing it.**

2. **After 24 hours, ask yourself: Do I still really want this?**

3. **If the answer is YES, buy it (if it fits within your budget).**

4. **If the answer is NO, congratulations—you just saved money!**

Why does this work?

- **Impulse buys** feel exciting at the moment, but waiting **gives your brain time to decide if it's truly worth it.**

- You'll often **realize you don't need the item** and can save your money for something better.

Waiting **just one day** before buying something can help you avoid **wasting money on things you don't actually need**.

4.3.4 The "One-Week Test" for Big Purchases

For **more significant purchases**, like a **video game, a new gadget, or a special outfit**, waiting **one whole week** before buying it is an excellent way to:

- **Make sure you really want it**

- **Compare prices and look for better deals**

- **Think about whether it fits into your budget**

Example:

- You see **a new skateboard for $80**. Instead of buying it immediately, you **wait a week**.
- After a week, you find **the same skateboard for $60 online**—saving **$20** just by waiting!

Waiting longer before making big purchases helps you find better deals and avoid regretful spending!

4.3.5 Delaying a Purchase for Something Bigger

Spending money is easy, but **spending money wisely** takes skill! Smart spending is about **getting the most value for your money**, avoiding wasteful purchases, and making sure your money is used to help **you reach your goals**.

In this section, we'll explore **how to make smart buying decisions, avoid impulse purchases, and develop spending habits that keep your wallet full while allowing you to enjoy life!**

What is Smart Spending?

Smart spending means making thoughtful money choices instead of buying something because it looks cool. It's about **understanding the difference between needs and wants, comparing prices, and ensuring you get the best deal**.

✔ Smart spenders don't just buy—they plan.

✔ They think about the long-term value of what they purchase.

✔ They look for ways to save money while getting what they need.

If you can learn **to spend wisely now**, you'll **always have enough money for what matters most!**

Comparing Prices: Always Look for the Best Deal!

Did you know the exact product can cost different amounts depending on where you buy it?

Smart spenders **always compare prices** to ensure they get the **best deal possible**.

Example: The Same Item, Different Prices!

You want to buy a **new book** that costs:

- **$20 at a bookstore**
- **$12 online**
- **$0 at the library!**

Which is the **smartest choice**?

Shopping around can help you **spend less while still getting what you want!**

Sales, Discounts, and Buying in Bulk: Spending Less, Getting More!

Smart shoppers use tricks to save money on things they buy regularly.

✔ **Buying in bulk** – Larger packages often **cost less per item** than smaller ones.

✔ **Using coupons or discount codes** – Can reduce the cost of your purchase.

✔ **Waiting for sales** – Some things go on **sale at certain times of the year** (for example, holiday sales).

Example: Smart Grocery Shopping

- A **small bag of chips** costs **$2.50** (single pack).
- A **big box with 10 small bags** costs **$15**—or **$1.50 per bag**.
- **Smart choice:** Buying the **bigger box saves you $1 per bag!**

Spending wisely doesn't mean **not buying things**—it means **buying them in a way that saves money**!

Try This: "Smart Shopper Challenge"

- Pick **one thing you want to buy** and compare its price in **three different places**.
- Find the **best deal** and see how much you save!

 ## 4.3.6 Key Takeaways

✔ **Financial independence means making smart money choices and planning ahead!**

✔ **Thinking before spending helps avoid impulse purchases and regrets.**

✔ **Mistakes are learning opportunities—use them to build better money habits!**

✔ **Taking responsibility for your money helps you feel in control of your financial future.**

✔ **Financial freedom starts with setting goals, planning, and sticking to smart money habits!**

 ### 4.3.7 Glossary

- **Financial Independence** – Being able to **manage your money wisely** so you can **make choices that support your future goals**.

- **Opportunity Cost** – The thing you **give up** when you choose to spend money on something else.

- **Budgeting Strategy** – A **personal plan for earning, spending, and saving money** to reach financial goals.

- **Delayed Gratification** – Waiting before buying something **so you can afford something even better later**.

- **Financial Freedom** – The ability to **make financial decisions based on what you want**, not just what you can afford.

Final Thoughts

Financial independence **starts now**—with the choices you make every day!

Imagine this:

- You **make smart spending choices** so you always have enough for what matters.

- You **learn from financial mistakes**, making each decision **better than the last**.

- You **set long-term goals and work toward them**, making your dreams a reality.

Your challenge: Create your own **Financial Freedom Plan** this month! List **three financial goals** and make a plan to **start working toward them today**.

4.4 Financial Responsibility

My Money, My Responsibility: Owning My Financial Future

Managing money is **not about being perfect**—it's about **learning, taking responsibility, and making choices that set you up for success.** Everyone, even adults, makes money mistakes, but **the smartest people learn from them.**

 ## 4.4.1 Learning Objectives

What You'll Learn in This Module:

- How to turn financial mistakes into lessons.
- Why taking charge of your money is YOUR responsibility.
- The three pillars of financial responsibility

(earning, managing, and growing money).

- **How to create a personal financial freedom plan.**

By the end of this section, you'll have the tools to **own your financial future and set yourself up for success!**

4.4.2 Learning from Financial Mistakes: Why It's Okay to Mess Up

Nobody always makes perfect money choices—even adults **make financial mistakes.** But remember, the key to **financial independence** is **not in avoiding mistakes, but in learning from them and making better decisions in the future. This knowledge empowers you to take control of your financial journey.**

Example

The Impulse Buy Regret

- You saw a **cool gadget at the store** and bought it right away.
- A week later, you **realized you didn't use it much** and wished you had **saved the money instead.**
- Next time, you **use the "Wait 7 Days" rule** to avoid making the same mistake.

Mistakes **aren't failures**—they're opportunities to **improve your money habits**!

Try This

"Fix My Money Mistake" Challenge

- Think about **a time you spent money and regretted it**.
- Write down **what you learned** from it.
- Make a plan for **what you'll do differently next time**.

4.4.3 My Money, My Responsibility: Owning My Financial Future

> **Who is responsible for your money?**
>
> **YOU ARE!**

Taking care of your money isn't just about saving and spending—it's about understanding that your financial future is in your hands. This understanding gives you a sense of control and security over your financial situation.

Nobody else will manage your money for you—so the sooner you learn to **take control, plan, and make smart choices, the better your future will be**.

Why Does This Matter?

✔ **Being responsible with money gives you freedom**—you can choose based on what you want, not what you can afford now.

✔ **Good money habits today = fewer money problems in the future.**

✔ **If you're responsible with money, you'll always have enough for what matters to you.**

The earlier you start taking responsibility for your money, the **easier it will be to reach your goals**!

4.4.4 The Three Pillars of Financial Responsibility

Managing money isn't just about spending—it's about **earning, managing, and growing money**. These three things help build a **strong financial future.**

1. **Earning Money**

    - You can't budget or save **if you don't have money to start with!** Learning how to **earn money** is the first step to financial success.

    - Ways to Earn Money as a Kid:

        • Doing **chores** for allowance,

        • Selling crafts or baked goods

        • Helping a neighbor with yard work.

2. **Managing Money**

    - **Once you earn money, you have to manage it wisely.** If you spend it all at once, you won't have any left for important things.

1. **Budgeting**

2. **Tracking expenses**

3. **Making thoughtful choices** about spending and saving.

4. **Growing Money**

    ◦ Money doesn't just sit there—it can **GROW** if you use it wisely!

    • **Saving money early** – means it has more time to grow.

    • **Investing money** – (when you're older) helps you build wealth.

    • **Earning interest** – on savings means your money makes money for you!

 Lesson

✔ The more you learn how to **earn money**, the more financial freedom you'll have!
✔ If you **don't manage your money, it will disappear quickly** —but if you **plan wisely, you'll always have enough for what matters most!**
✔The sooner you start **saving and growing money, the more you'll have in the future!**

4.4.5 Financial Freedom: Creating My Money Plan

What is financial freedom? It's when you have **enough money to make choices based on what YOU want**, not just what you can afford at the moment.

The Three Steps to Financial Freedom

1. **Know Your Money** – Track your income, spending, and savings.

2. **Set Goals for the Future** – Plan ahead, whether it's a **big purchase, education, or experience**!

3. **Make Smart Money Decisions** – Every financial choice you make today **affects your future freedom**!

Example

The 5-Year Money Plan

Imagine where you want to be in **5 years**. What do you want to afford?

- A **car**?
- A **big trip**?

What steps can you take today to get closer to that goal?

Financial freedom comes from making small, smart money choices every day!

Try This: "My Money Freedom Plan" Worksheet

- Write down **3 financial goals for the next 5 years**.
- List **steps you can take now** to start achieving them.

 ## 4.4.6 Key Takeaways

Taking Charge of Your Financial Future!

✔ **Financial independence** means making smart money choices and planning ahead!

✔ **Thinking before spending** helps avoid impulse purchases and regrets.

✔ **Mistakes are learning opportunities**—use them to build better money habits!

✔ **Taking responsibility for your money** helps you feel in control of your financial future.

✔ **Financial freedom starts with setting goals, planning, and sticking to smart money habits!**

 ## 4.4.7 Glossary

- **Financial Independence** – Being able to **manage your money wisely** so you can **make choices that support your future goals**.

- **Opportunity Cost** – The thing you **give up** when you choose to spend money on something else.

- **Budgeting Strategy** – A **personal plan for earning, spending, and saving money** to reach financial goals.

- **Delayed Gratification** – Waiting before buying something **so you can afford something even better later.**

- **Financial Freedom** – The ability to **make financial decisions based on what you want**, not just on what you can afford at the moment.

Final Thoughts

Financial independence **starts now**—with the choices you make every day!

Imagine this:

- You **make smart spending choices** so you always have enough for what matters.

- You **learn from financial mistakes**, making each decision **better than the last.**

- You **set long-term goals and work toward them**, making your dreams a reality.

Your challenge: Create your own **Financial Freedom Plan** this month! List **three financial goals** and make a plan to **start working toward them today!**

Keep Going!

If something doesn't make sense right away, that's okay! You can:

- **Review a section**
- **Ask a parent or teacher for help**
- **Try a hands-on activity**

Every step you take brings you closer to being a money-smart pro! **Keep learning, exploring, and having fun with money!**

Transition to Module 5: Giving & Growing Your Money

Now that you've learned how to **spend wisely**, you're well on your way to becoming a money master! But managing money isn't just about earning, saving, and spending—it's also about using it to **make a difference** and **help it grow**.

In **Module 5**, we'll explore two powerful ways to use your money:
Giving – How sharing your money can help others and bring joy.
Investing – How money can grow over time and work for you!

Get ready to discover how to **give with purpose** and **build wealth for the future**!

MODULE 5
FAMILY FINANCE ADVENTURES - LESSONS FOR THE WHOLE FAMILY

5.1 Family Financial Fitness

Making Money a Fun Family Conversation!

Have you ever played a game where you had to guess the price of something? It's fun to test your knowledge and see who has the best money sense! Now, imagine playing that game with your family—not just for fun, but to **learn more about how money works together**.

Money is a **massive part of life**, and the more you **understand it,** together as a **family, the stronger your financial future will be**! However, it's important to acknowledge that discussing money can sometimes be challenging due to differing opinions and emotions. We'll provide you with strategies to navigate these challenges and make your money conversations more productive.

5.1.1 Learning Objectives

By the end of this section, you will:

- Learn how to start fun and easy **money conversations with your family.**

- Discover the best ways to work together to make **smart financial choices.**

- Understand how family stories and experiences can teach **valuable money lessons.**

- Create a **Family Financial Communication Toolkit** to make money talks easier!

5.1.2 Why Talking About Money is Important

> **Did you know that families discussing money openly are more likely to make smarter financial choices together?**

As parents, you play a crucial role in shaping your children's financial habits. By discussing money openly and making smart financial choices, you set a good example for your children. Many kids feel **left out of money discussions**—but the more you **learn and participate**, the better prepared you'll be for the future.

Talking about money with your family **helps you:**

- Understand where money comes from and where it goes
- Learn how to budget, save, and make good spending choices
- Avoid money mistakes before you make them
- Work as a team to plan for big goals like vacations or saving for something special

Money affects everyone in a family—the more you talk about it, the easier it becomes to **make smart financial choices together**!

5.1.3 Fun Ways to Start Money Conversations with Your Family

How do you bring up money in a family conversation? Try these fun ideas!

Play "Guess the Price!" – A Fun Family Money Game

- Pick five household items (like a box of cereal, a movie ticket, or a pair of shoes).
- Each person guesses the price, and the closest guess wins a point!
- Talk about which items were more expensive than expected and why.

Lesson: This game helps you understand how much things cost and why budgeting matters!

Use Conversation Starter Cards!

Use these fun money-related questions to start a discussion at the dinner table:

- "What would you do if you found $20 on the street?"
- "What's something you REALLY want to save for?"
- "Would you rather get a $50 gift now or $100 in a year?"
- "What's the smartest money decision you've ever made?"

Lesson: Talking about money can be **fun** when you ask the right questions!

Family Money Story Time! – Learning From Real-Life Experiences

Your parents, grandparents, and older siblings have learned good and bad money lessons, and sharing these experiences can be incredibly valuable. It's a chance for parents to pass on their knowledge and for children to learn from their family's real-life experiences. Ask your family:

- What was the first thing you ever saved for?
- Did you ever waste money on something you regretted?
- What was your best financial decision?

Example:

- Mom might tell you about how she saved for her first bike.
- Grandpa might share how he made a money mistake and what he learned from it.

Lesson: Learning from **family stories** can help you **avoid mistakes and develop smart money habits early!**

5.1.4 Working Together as a Family to Make Smart Money Choices

Families make financial decisions together all the time! From planning vacations to grocery shopping, money choices affect everyone in a household.

How Can Kids Help With Family Money Decisions?

- **Helping with grocery budgeting** – Compare prices and look for the best deals.
- **Planning for a family trip** – Help determine the best way to save.
- **Cutting down on unnecessary expenses** – Turn off lights, avoid food waste, and be mindful of spending.

By involving children in family financial decisions, you not only lighten the parents' load but also teach children valuable money management skills. This early exposure to financial decision-making can help them develop a sense of responsibility and prepare them for their own financial independence.

Lesson: Even as a kid, **you can contribute to smart family money choices**, which helps prepare you for the future!

5.1.5 Building a Family Financial Communication Toolkit

Just like a toolkit helps fix things, a financial communication toolkit helps families talk about money better. It's a way to stay organized, prepared, and on the same page when it comes to financial discussions and decisions.

What's in a Family Money Toolkit?

- **A Financial Vocabulary List** – Learn words like budget, saving, investing, and expenses so money talks make sense!

- **A "How to Talk About Money" Guide** – Tips like asking questions, listening carefully, and being patient.

- **A Family Financial Goal Sheet** – Write down what your family wants to save for and track progress together!

Lesson: When everyone understands money terms and goals, working as a team makes smart financial decisions easier!

5.1.6 Key Takeaways

✔ Talking about money with family **helps everyone make smarter choices!**

✔ Fun games and conversation starters make **discussing money easier.**

✔ Learning from family money stories helps **avoid financial mistakes.**

✔ **Kids can help with real money decisions**—like budgeting and saving!

✔ **A Family Financial Toolkit** makes money discussions simple and fun!

5.1.7 Glossary: Family Financial Terms

- **Budget** – A plan for how much money you will save, spend, and give each month.

- **Smart Spending** – Making choices that help you get the most value for your money.

- **Financial Goal** – Something you want to save money for, like a trip, a bike, or college.

- **Opportunity Cost** – The thing you give up when you choose to spend money on something else.

- **Financial Responsibility** – Understanding that **YOU** are in control of your money choices and that planning ahead helps you make better decisions.

Final Thoughts

Money Talks = Family Teamwork!

- Your family **works together to plan vacations, big purchases, and savings goals.**
- You feel **confident asking questions about money and sharing your own ideas!**
- You and your parents **make smart money decisions together**—helping everyone **save more and spend wisely!**

Your challenge: Start a money conversation with your family this week! Use one of the **conversation starters, play "Guess the Price," or help with a family financial decision!**

5.2 The Family Budget

Planning Together

Managing money isn't just for adults—**families that plan their budgets together make smarter financial choices**! A family budget meeting is like a team huddle before a big game. Everyone comes together to set financial goals, track spending, and ensure money is used wisely.

 ### 5.2.1 Learning Objectives

By the end of this section, you will:

- How to hold a fun and productive **family budget meeting**
- Understanding **household expenses and why budgets matter**

- How **kids can participate in family budgeting**
- Setting **family financial goals and working toward them together**

5.2.2 Why Families Should Budget Together

 Did you know? Families that talk openly about money make better financial choices and feel less stressed about money!

A family budget meeting **helps everyone:**

- Know where the money goes (bills, groceries, savings, fun, etc.)
- Set shared financial goals (saving for a trip, buying a new pet, or fixing up the house)
- Find ways to save money together
- Make money discussions normal and easy

Lesson: Budgeting as a family teaches teamwork, responsibility, and smart money habits for life!

5.2.3 How to Hold a Fun and Productive Family Budget Meeting

A budget meeting shouldn't feel like a boring school lecture—it can be fun, interactive, and engaging for everyone!

Step 1: Set a Time & Place

- Choose a monthly budget meeting time (for example, the first Saturday of the month).
- Have snacks and drinks to make it feel casual and fun.

Step 2: Create a Budget Team Mindset!

- Think of your family as a money team —everyone plays a role in reaching financial goals!
- Kids can contribute ideas, track spending, or suggest money-saving ways.

Step 3: Review Monthly Income & Expenses

- Parents share how much money is coming in (income) and how much is being spent (expenses).
- Discuss different spending categories (bills, food, savings, fun).
- Kids can help track spending on specific categories like entertainment or eating out.

Step 4: Plan for Upcoming Expenses

- Are any big purchases or expenses coming up? (Birthdays, holidays, vacations?)
- Talk about budgeting for those ahead of time instead of waiting until the last minute.

Step 5: Set a Family Financial Goal

- Decide on one big savings goal (for example, saving for a family trip, a new pet, or a game console).
- Everyone contributes by finding ways to save money toward the goal.

Lesson: When budgeting feels like a team effort, everyone is more motivated to make smart money choices!

5.2.4 Understanding Household Expenses: Where Does the Money Go?

Why can't we buy whatever we want all the time? Because families have **expenses** that must be covered first.

Basic Household Expenses Include:

- **Housing (Rent/Mortgage)** – Keeping a roof over our heads!
- **Utilities (Electricity, Water, Internet)** – Paying for what we use daily.
- **Groceries & Food** – Keeping the fridge full!
- **Transportation** – Gas, car payments, or bus tickets.
- **Savings & Emergency Funds** – Preparing for unexpected situations.

Fun vs. Essential Expenses

- **Essential expenses** (bills, groceries) must be paid first.

- **Fun expenses** (movies, eating out) can be adjusted if needed.

Example:

- If a family spends $200 monthly on eating out, could they cut it to $100 and save the other $100 for a trip?
- This is how smart budgeting helps families reach goals faster!

Lesson: Understanding **household expenses** helps kids understand why parents sometimes **say no to extra spending**—it's not about being unfair; it's about making sure the family's needs are met first.

5.2.5 How Kids Can Help With Family Budgeting

Children can play a significant role in family budgeting. They can help by tracking spending, comparing store prices, contributing to savings goals, and suggesting cost-cutting measures. Their active involvement can make budgeting a family affair.

- **Tracking spending**: Help list expenses and see where money is going.
- **Comparing prices at the store** – Find cheaper options or discounts.
- **Helping with savings goals** – Contribute part of your allowance toward a family goal.
- **Finding ways to cut costs** – Suggest free activities instead of expensive outings.

Example

The Grocery Shopping Challenge!

Your family has a **$100** grocery budget.

- Your challenge? **Find ways to buy everything needed while saving money.**
- Look for **discounts, compare brands, and add up costs as you shop!**

Lesson: Budgeting isn't just for adults—kids can **actively manage money wisely, and it's empowering!**

5.2.6 Setting Family Financial Goals & Tracking Progress

Setting and tracking family financial goals is a great way to make budgeting more engaging and rewarding. It's like embarking on a financial adventure together, with each step bringing the family closer to their goal.

Examples of Family Savings Goals:

- Saving for a vacation
- Buying a new pet
- Upgrading household items (like a TV or gaming console)
- Saving for special experiences (concerts, amusement parks, road trips)

How to Track Progress:

- **Use a savings chart** – Color in sections as the family gets closer to the goal!

- **Set a deadline** – Pick a date for when you want to reach the goal.

- **Find ways to add to savings** – Can everyone contribute a little each month?

Lesson: Working toward a goal together makes budgeting more exciting and rewarding!

 ## 5.2.7 Key Takeaways

Family Budgeting = Teamwork and Unity!

✔ **Family budgeting** helps everyone understand where **money goes and how to spend wisely.**

✔ **Kids can be part of financial decisions** by tracking expenses and helping with savings goals.

✔ A family budget meeting makes planning money **fun and interactive!**

✔ **Understanding expenses** helps explain why families must prioritize spending.

✔ **Setting and tracking** financial goals as a family helps make dreams a reality!

 ## 5.2.8 Glossary: Family Budgeting Terms

Budget Meeting – A family discussion about money, expenses, and financial goals.

- **Household Expenses** – The costs of running a home, like rent, food, and utilities.

- **Financial Goal** – A big savings target for something the family wants (like a vacation or pet).

- **Smart Spending** – Finding ways to save money by choosing budget-friendly options.

Final Thoughts

Budgeting Together = A Stronger Family!

Imagine this:

- Your family **works together to plan vacations, big purchases, and savings goals.**

- You **understand where money goes** and why budgeting is essential.

- You **feel confident contributing ideas** and helping make smart financial decisions!

Your challenge: Ask your parents about your family budget! See if you can help track expenses, compare prices, or suggest a savings goal!

5.3 Family Savings Goal

Teamwork Makes the Dream Work

Saving money isn't just something **individuals do**—families can work toward big financial goals together! Whether saving for a **vacation, a new pet, a home upgrade, or a fun family experience**, working as a team makes saving **more fun, achievable, and meaningful**.

5.3.1 Learning Objectives

By the end of this section, you will:

- Understand how to **set a shared savings goal as a family**.

- Discover ways **everyone—kids and parents—can contribute**.

- **Use visual trackers** to keep savings fun and exciting.

- **Celebrate milestones** along the way to stay motivated.

5.3.2 How to Set a Family Savings Goal

A great family savings goal should be something everyone is excited about!

Step 1: Have a Goal-Setting Meeting

Gather as a family and **brainstorm ideas**. What's something **everyone** would love to save for?

Some ideas might be:

- A beach vacation
- A new family pet
- A big backyard project (like a treehouse!)
- A new gaming console or home entertainment system
- A memorable holiday experience (like Disneyland or a ski trip)

Step 2: Decide on a Goal That's Realistic & Exciting

Once you've picked a goal, make sure it's:

- **Specific** – Example: "Save $1,000 for a beach vacation by next summer."
- **Achievable** – The goal should be big enough to be exciting but realistic enough to reach.

- **Agreed upon by everyone** – Everyone should feel excited about working toward it!

Lesson: A clear, exciting savings goal **motivates the family** to work together!

5.3.3 Creative Ways for Families to Save Money Together

Saving as a family means everyone pitches in! Here are some creative ways to contribute:

Start a "Family Savings Challenge"

- Each person sets a savings goal based on their allowance, earnings, or extra chores.
- **Example**: If a child saves $5 a week and a parent saves $50, it all adds up fast!
- Use a chart or tracker (see next section) to motivate everyone.

Have a "Spare Change Jar"

- Keep a family piggy bank or jar where everyone can drop extra coins they find or save.
- Every month, count it together and add it to the savings goal!

Cut Back on Small Expenses & Save the Difference

- If your family usually eats out once a week, try eating out less and putting that money into savings.

Example: Skipping one $40 restaurant meal per month = $480 saved in a year!

Find Ways to Earn Extra Money as a Family

- Have a **garage sale** to sell old toys, clothes, or books.
- Start a **small family business** (like selling baked goods, crafts, or car washes).
- Kids can **help with household chores** to earn and contribute money.

Lesson: When everyone contributes—even in small ways—the savings grow faster, and the goal feels more achievable!

5.3.4 Making Savings Fun: How to Track Progress Together!

Watching your savings grow keeps everyone motivated!

Create a Savings Goal Chart

- Draw a **big progress tracker** on paper and **hang it on the fridge**.
- As you save money, **color in sections** to show how close you are to the goal!

Use a Digital Tracker or App

If your family prefers technology, use an app like:

- **Greenlight** (lets families set savings goals together)

- **PiggyBot** (a fun savings app for kids)

Have a Family "Savings Countdown"

- Write down how much money is **left to save**, and update it weekly.
- Each time you reach a small milestone, **celebrate the progress**!

Lesson: Seeing visual progress helps the whole family stay excited and motivated!

5.3.5 Celebrating Milestones: The Key to Staying Motivated!

Big goals take time—so celebrating small wins keeps the excitement alive!

How to Celebrate Savings Milestones

- Have a **mini celebration** every time you save **25%, 50%, or 75% of the goal**
- Do something fun but inexpensive—like a **movie night or special family meal**
- Give each family member a **small reward** for their contributions

Example: Saving for a Beach Trip!

- At **25% saved**, → Have a "beach night" at home with towels and tropical music!

- At **50% saved**, → Play a beach trivia game together!
- At **75% saved**, → Plan what you'll pack for the trip together!

Lesson: Celebrating along the way **keeps everyone excited** and makes the journey fun!

5.3.6 Overcoming Challenges: What If Someone Can't Contribute?

Not everyone can contribute the same amount—but everyone can still be part of the team!

What to Do If Someone Can't Contribute Financially:

- **Find other ways to help!** If a sibling can't contribute money, they can **help organize the budget or find discounts**
- **Encourage effort, not just dollars!** If someone **earns $5 but gives $1**, that's still fantastic teamwork!
- **Stay positive!** Remind everyone that **every little bit counts!**

Lesson: Even if someone can't contribute money, they can contribute effort—everyone plays a role in reaching the goal!

5.3.7 Key Takeaways

Saving as a Family = Teamwork!

✔ **Setting a shared savings goal as a family** makes money management exciting!

✔ There are many **creative ways to save together**—small amounts add up!

✔ **Tracking progress visually** keeps everyone engaged and motivated.

✔ **Celebrating small milestones** makes reaching the goal more fun!

✔ **Even if someone can't contribute money, they can help in other ways.**

5.3.8 Glossary: Family Savings Terms

- **Savings Goal** – A target amount of money a family wants to save for something special.

- **Progress Tracker** – A chart or app that helps families see how much they've saved.

- **Milestone** – A small savings achievement along the way to the final goal.

- **Team Savings Challenge** – A fun way to get everyone involved in reaching the family goal!

Final Thoughts

Imagine this:

- Your family sets a goal and works as a team to achieve it.

- Everyone feels involved and excited about reaching a shared dream.

- You all learn valuable lessons about money, patience, and teamwork!

Your challenge: Talk to your family about **setting a savings goal together**—see what you can all work toward as a team!

5.4 The Grocery Store Game: Comparing Prices with Famil4

Turning Grocery Shopping Into a Fun Learning Adventure!

Have you ever wondered why two cereal brands cost different amounts or more oversized packages? Sometimes, they cost less per unit than smaller ones.

 ### 5.4.1 Learning Objectives

By the end of this section, you will:

- **Compare prices** to find the best deal
- **Understand unit pricing** and why it matters
- **Spot marketing tricks** that make people spend more money

- **Work as a family** to stick to a grocery budget

5.4.2 Why Comparing Prices is a Superpower

 **Did you know that two products that look the same can have very different prices?**

Many people buy things without checking if they're getting the best deal. Stores use clever tricks to make you spend more than you need to. But here's the secret: **smart shoppers know how to compare prices** and find the best value, putting you in control of your spending!

- **Bigger isn't always cheaper!** Sometimes, a smaller package costs less per unit than a big one.

- **Sales aren't always a good deal!** Some "discounts" only slightly lower the price, but the item is still expensive.

- **Store brands vs. name brands** – Many store brands taste the same but cost much less!

Remember, the more you pay attention to prices, the more money you and your family can save! This is a practical skill that can be applied every time you shop.

5.4.3 The Power of Unit Pricing: A Secret Tool for Smart Shoppers!

What is unit pricing? It tells you how much something costs per ounce, pound, or item instead of the total price.

Example: Two Boxes of Cereal

Brand	Size	Total Price	Unit Price (per ounce)
Brand A	12 oz	$3.60	$0.30 per oz
Brand B	20 oz	$5.00	$0.25 per oz

Which one is the better deal? **Brand B**, because you get more cereal for each dollar spent!

Try This

"Find the Best Unit Price" Game!

- At the store, pick two sizes of the same product (milk, cereal, or chips).
- Divide the total price by the weight or number of items to find the unit price.
- See which one gives you the most for your money!

Unit pricing is a powerful tool that helps you compare prices fairly and avoid overpaying. It's a key aspect of smart shopping!

5.4.4 The Grocery Store Game: How to Play!

Turn grocery shopping into a fun competition with your family!

Step 1: Set the Rules

- Pick a budget for a specific category (ex: "Snacks – $10 Max").
- Each person finds the best deal using unit pricing.

- The goal is to get the most value for the money!

Step 2: Compare Prices & Look for Deals

- Check price tags for unit pricing—this is key to finding the best deal.
- Look for sales, coupons, and store brand options.
- Watch out for tricky packaging! (Sometimes a "Family Size" is more expensive per unit).

Step 3: Add It Up & See Who Wins!

- The winner is the person who got the most value while staying within budget!
- Discuss as a family: What surprised you? Where did you save the most?

Lesson: Comparing prices is a powerful skill that helps families save money!

5.4.5 Marketing Tricks That Make You Spend More!

Stores use clever strategies to get you to spend more money without realizing it.

Top Marketing Tricks to Watch Out For:

- **"Buy One, Get One 50% Off"** – Sounds like a deal, but if you only need one item, you might spend more than you planned.

- **Product Placement** – Expensive items are placed at eye level so you see them first. Cheaper options are often on lower or higher shelves!

- **Big Shopping Carts** – Stores make carts bigger so you feel like you haven't bought much yet, which makes you buy more!

- **Checkout Impulse Buys** – Candy, magazines, and drinks are placed at checkout to tempt you into last-minute spending!

Lesson: Knowing these tricks helps avoid overspending and stick to your budget, making you a more financially responsible shopper!

5.4.6 Key Takeaways

Grocery Shopping Like a Pro!

✔ Comparing prices helps you find the **best deals and avoid overpaying.**

✔ Unit pricing tells you how much something **costs per ounce, pound, or item—use it to compare prices fairly!**

✔ Stores use tricks to make you spend more—**watch out for sneaky sales and product placement.**

✔ A Grocery Savings Jar Challenge **helps track how much you save as a family!**

 ## 5.4.7 Glossary: Grocery Store Smart Shopping Terms

- **Unit Pricing** – The cost of an item per unit (ounce, pound, liter) so you can compare prices fairly.

- **Budget Shopping** – Ensure you don't spend more than planned at the store.

- **Price Comparison** – Looking at different brands and sizes to find the best value.

- **Impulse Buys** – Things you buy last-minute without planning, often near the checkout.

Final Thoughts

Grocery Shopping is a Superpower!

- You **find the best deals** and **help your family save money**.

- You **understand marketing tricks** and don't fall for expensive impulse buys.

- You **use smart shopping strategies** to get more value for every dollar spent.

Your challenge: Next time you go grocery shopping, play The Grocery Store Game with your family and see how much you can save!

5.5 The Financial Quiz: Test Your Money Skill Knowledge!

Are You a Money Master? Let's Find Out!

Throughout this book, you've learned about **earning, saving, budgeting, spending wisely, and making smart financial decisions**. Now, it's time to put your knowledge to the test with **The Financial Quiz!**

5.5.1 Learning Objectives

By the end of this section, you will:

- **Test your financial knowledge** in a fun and interactive way.

- **Work as a team or challenge yourself** to be a Money Master.

- **Discover areas where you can** strengthen your financial knowledge.

5.5.2 How to Play The Financial Quiz

You can play this quiz solo or as a family! Choose the best way to play:

- **Solo Mode** – Answer the questions on your own and keep track of your score.

- **Team Mode** – Compete with friends or family members. The person with the highest score wins!

- **Challenge Mode** – Take turns explaining WHY your answer is correct—great for deeper learning!

Scoring System

- **+2 points** for every correct answer

- **+1 bonus point** if you explain WHY your answer is correct

- **0 points** if you get it wrong (but you'll learn something new!)

5.5.3 Financial Quiz Questions

Level 1: Money Basics

1. What is the main purpose of a budget?

A) To keep track of how much candy you eat

B) To plan how you earn, save, and spend money wisely

C) To make sure you spend all your money as fast as possible

D) To guess how much money you have

2. Which is the best definition of "income"?

A) Money you borrow from friends

B) Money you receive (like allowance, gifts, or earnings)

C) Money you find on the ground

D) Money that disappears when you spend it

3. What does "saving money" mean?

A) Hiding money under your bed

B) Using money only for emergencies

C) Setting aside money for future needs or goals

D) Spending money as soon as you get it

Level 2: Smart Spending & Budgeting

4. How much do you have left if you earn $50 and spend $40?

A) $90

B) $10

C) $50

D) $0

5. What is an example of an "impulse purchase"?

A) Buying something you planned for in advance

B) Buying something just because it looks cool, without thinking

C) Saving up for something over time

D) Comparing prices before buying

6. What does "opportunity cost" mean?

A) The thing you didn't choose when making a money decision

B) The cost of buying a new opportunity

C) A special price you get when shopping online

D) A discount on expensive items

Level 3: Advanced Money Skills

7. What is "compound interest"?

A) When interest earns more interest over time

B) When you spend all your money at once

C) A game about money

D) When you only earn interest on your original savings

8. What's the best reason to have an emergency fund?

A) To spend on fun things when you feel like it

B) To have money set aside for unexpected expenses

C) To buy gifts for friends

D) To lend money to people

9. Why is it important to compare prices before buying something?

A) To spend more money

B) To make sure you're getting the best deal

C) Because stores like when you take a long time to shop

D) To show off how much you know about money

Bonus Challenge Questions!

- **Would you rather have $100 today or $200 in a year?** Why?

- **If you found $20 on the street, what would you do with it?**

- **What's the best money advice you've ever learned?**

5.5.4 What Did You Learn? Reflection & Discussion

Great job! Whether you got every question right or learned something new, you're on your way to becoming a Money Master!

Discussion Questions:

- What was the hardest question, and why?

- Which money skill do you want to get better at?

- How can you use what you learned today in real life?

Lesson: Sharing and discussing your financial knowledge **helps you learn and remember financial lessons better**, and your insights are valuable!

5.5.5 Create Your Own Financial Quiz!

Now it's your turn! Write your own quiz questions and test your family or friends.

- Come up with 5 money-related questions.
- Write down the correct answers and 3 "trick" answers.
- Challenge someone to take your quiz!

Lesson: Teaching others **is one of the best ways to learn**!

5.5.6 Key Takeaways

✔ Quizzes help you test your **money knowledge in a fun way!**

✔ Explaining your answers helps you remember **key financial skills.**

✔ **Learning about money** is easier when it's interactive and engaging.

✔ Creating your own quiz is a **great way to challenge yourself and others!**

5.5.7 Glossary: Financial Quiz Terms

- **Budget** – A plan for how much money you will save, spend, and give each month.

- **Compound Interest** – Interest that earns more interest over time, helping savings grow faster.

- **Emergency Fund** – Money set aside for unexpected expenses like car repairs or medical bills.

- **Opportunity Cost** – The thing you give up when you

choose to spend money on something else.

Final Thoughts

Test Your Skills & Keep Learning!

- You **understand money concepts better than most adults!**
- You can **help others make smart financial decisions**.
- You're on your way to **financial independence and freedom!**

Your challenge: Take the quiz with a family member or friend—see who gets the highest score!

Financial Quiz With Answers!

No Cheating

Level 1: Money Basics

1. What is the main purpose of a budget?
 B) To plan how you earn, save, and spend money wisely

2. Which is the best definition of "income"?
 B) Money you receive (like allowance, gifts, or earnings)

3. What does "saving money" mean?
 C) Setting aside money for future needs or goals

Level 2: Smart Spending & Budgeting

4. If you earn $50 and spend $40, how much do you have left?
 B) $10

5. What is an example of an "impulse purchase"?
 B) Buying something just because it looks cool, without thinking

6. What does "opportunity cost" mean?
A) The thing you didn't choose when making a money decision

Level 3: Advanced Money Skills

7. What is "compound interest"?
A) When interest earns more interest over time

8. What's the best reason to have an emergency fund?
B) To have money set aside for unexpected expenses

9. Why is it important to compare prices before buying something?
B) To make sure you're getting the best deal

Bonus Challenge Questions!

- **Would you rather have $100 today or $200 in a year?** Why? (Best answer: $200 in a year, because waiting and saving lets your money grow!)

- **If you found $20 on the street, what would you do with it?** (Best answer: Save it, donate it, or spend it wisely!)

- **What's the best money advice you've ever learned?** (Your own answer!)

Keeping the Journey Going

Now that you've explored the world of money, savings, and smart spending, you have the tools to make great financial choices! But learning about money isn't just for you—it's something we can share with others.

By leaving a quick review on Amazon, you'll help other parents, teachers, and kids find this book and start their own journey to financial confidence.

Your review is like a guiding light, showing families where they can find fun and easy ways to learn about money. Whether you loved the interactive activities, the engaging stories, or the helpful lessons, your honest opinion makes a big difference!

How to Leave a Review

It's easy! Just scan the QR code below or visit this link: https://www.amazon.com/review/review-your-purchases/?asin=BOOKASIN

Write a few sentences about what you liked—maybe your favorite lesson or activity!

Thank you for being part of this mission. Financial literacy grows stronger when we share what we've learned—and you're helping to make that happen!

Conclusion

Wow, what a journey we've been on together! This book covers so much, from the basics of money to becoming a money master. Let's quickly look at all the great things we've learned.

We embarked on this journey with the joy of learning about money—what it is, where it comes from, and why it's essential. We played games and told stories to make learning about coins, bills, and savings a thrilling adventure. This joy of learning made our journey exciting and engaging. Then, we moved on to building smart money habits, like setting goals, creating budgets, and being savvy shoppers. You learned how to grow your money by saving and even starting a small business!

As we progressed, we tackled more significant money concepts, like distinguishing between needs and wants, making tough choices, and being responsible with our cash. We discussed becoming a money boss by planning, staying organized, and learning from our mistakes. You discovered the power of working together with your family on financial matters and how to be a money-smart kid in the real world.

But the best part? You learned that money is a tool you can use to make your dreams come true. Whether you want to save up for something special, help others, or change the world, the money skills you've gained will help you achieve those goals. You've got the power to take charge of your financial future, and that's pretty awesome.

So, why does all this money knowledge matter? It's not just knowledge; it's power. Being good with money is like having a superpower. It allows you to do more of what you love, help the people you care about, and live the life you want. When you know how to manage your money, you're in control. You can make smart choices, solve problems, and feel confident about your future. This power is in your hands, and it's yours to wield.

However, learning about money isn't a one-time thing. It's a lifelong adventure! There's always more to discover and explore. Keep practicing what you've learned, and don't hesitate to ask questions. Talk to your family about money, play money games with your friends, and look for ways to apply your real-life skills. Remember, the more you practice, the better you'll become. So keep at it, and never stop learning!

Here's a challenge: pick one money goal to work on, like saving up for a special toy or learning how to budget your allowance. Create a plan and involve your family in the process. See how far you can go and celebrate your successes along the way. Remember, every little step counts!

As we wrap up this money adventure, I want you to know how proud I am of you. You've learned and grown in ways you might not even realize. The money skills you've gained will stick with you as you grow up and take on new challenges. You have what it takes to be a money master!

So here's my final piece of advice: believe in yourself. You can shape your financial future and turn your dreams into reality. Keep learning, growing, and being the fantastic, money-smart kid you are. The world is waiting for you!

Thank you for joining me on this exciting journey through the world of money. It's been a pleasure sharing these lessons and watching you grow. Remember, you've got a money coach and a friend in me. Whenever you need help or encouragement, I'm here for you. You're not alone in this journey, and I'm always here to support you.

Now, go out there and show the world what a money master looks like! I can't wait to see all the fantastic things you'll accomplish. Keep shining, keep dreaming, and keep being awesome!

Your money coach and biggest fan,

Rachael Miller

References

1. Best budget apps for families (2025): 7 tools to manage .... (n.d.). Retrieved from https://marriagekidsandmoney.com/best-budget-apps-for-families/

2. Budgeting for kids: How to teach it and why it matters. (n.d.). Retrieved from https://www.thebalancemoney.com/teach-kids-to-budget-money-454012

3. Budgeting game | Money Games for Kids – MoneySense. (n.d.). Retrieved from https://natwest.mymoneysense.com/students/students-8-12/the-budget-game/

4. Children's books that teach financial lessons. (n.d.). Retrieved from https://treasurer.mo.gov/financial-literacy/patchildrensbooks

5. Comparison shopping tips. (n.d.). Retrieved from https://snapedny.org/tip-sheets/comparison-shopping-tips/

6. Dollars & sense: Money management for kids. (n.d.). Retrieved from https://www.scholastic.com/parents/family-life/financial-literacy/dollars-and-sense-money-management-kids.html

7. Effective strategies for teaching decision-making to elementary students. (n.d.). Retrieved from https://everydayspeech.com/blog-posts/general/effective-strategies-for-teaching-decision-making-to-elementary-students/

8. Eighteen fun money activities for kids. (n.d.). Retrieved from https://www.gohenry.com/us/blog/financial-education/18-fun-money-activities-for-kids

9. Family financial education resources & activities | CEE. (n.d.). Retrieved from https://www.councilforeconed.org/programs/for-families/

10. Financial glossary for kids broken down by age. (n.d.). Retrieved from https://www.csefcu.com/blog/post/financial-glossary-for-kids-broken-down-by-age

11. Financial milestones for kids: An age-by-age guide. (n.d.). Retrieved from https://www.gohenry.com/us/blog/financial-education/financial-milestones-for-kids-an-age-by-age-guid

12. Four steps to goal setting for kids – free printable. (n.d.). Retrieved from https://scholarwithin.com/successful-goal-setting-for-kids?srsltid=AfmBOopaaklO_xAqVAv4qWTYsQFrrV

XiLthNNbXaA5TmGVLQL23VwWZ

13. Fourteen teen entrepreneurs and how they succeeded. (n.d.). Retrieved from https://www.oxford-royale.com/articles/14-teen-entrepreneurs

14. Fun ways to teach kids entrepreneurship. (n.d.). Retrieved from https://kidpreneurs.org/fun-ways-to-teach-kids-entrepreneurship/

15. How household chores shape children's financial attitudes. (n.d.). Retrieved from https://lebaron-black.byu.edu/money-and-laundering-how-household-chores-shape-childrens-financial-attitudes

16. How to earn money as a kid: Detailed steps and tips. (n.d.). Retrieved from https://craftulate.com/how-to-earn-money-as-a-kid/

17. How to teach the difference between wants and needs. (n.d.). Retrieved from https://elementaryedu.com/2022/07/the-difference-between-wants-and-needs.html

18. How to teach kids budgeting: A simple guide for parents. (n.d.). Retrieved from https://www.primewayfcu.com/blog/teach-kids-budgeting-skills

19. How to teach needs vs wants for kids & teens. (n.d.). Retrieved from https://www.mydoh.ca/learn/blog/education/how-to-teach-kids-teens-the-difference-between-needs-vs-

wants/

20. How to teach your kids about: emergency funds. (n.d.). Retrieved from https://www.bluetreesavings.com/post/how-to-teach-your-kids-about-emergency-funds

21. Introducing the "wealth whiz quiz" mini-game for your ... (n.d.). Retrieved from https://www.personalfinancelab.com/blog/introducing-the-wealth-whiz-quiz-mini-game-for-your-students/

22. Let kids try the 52-week savings challenge. (n.d.). Retrieved from https://www.lgfcu.org/personal-finance/let-kids-try-the-52-week-savings-challenge

23. Money and finance: History of money. (n.d.). Retrieved from https://www.ducksters.com/money/history_of_money.php

24. Money games for kids – MoneySense. (n.d.). Retrieved from https://natwest.mymoneysense.com/parents/games-interactives/

25. Online games and apps that teach kids about money. (n.d.). Retrieved from https://dfi.wa.gov/financial-education/educators/online-games-and-apps

26. Teachers: How storytelling can help teach financial literacy. (n.d.). Retrieved from https://yourmoneyvehicle.com/teachers/teachers-st

orytelling/

27. Team nutrition popular events idea booklet. (n.d.). Retrieved from https://fns-prod.azureedge.us/sites/default/files/resource-files/tn-events-shopsmart.pdf

28. These fun games can teach your kids about money. (n.d.). Retrieved from https://www.cnbc.com/2021/01/14/these-fun-games-can-teach-your-kids-about-money.html

29. The ultimate list of children's books to spark financial responsibility early. (n.d.). Retrieved from https://www.radixfinancial.com/blog/ultimate-list-childrens-books-spark-financial-responsibility-early

30. Uncovering the history of coins: Fascinating facts and stories – Tomas Hensrud Gulla. (n.d.). Retrieved from https://www.gulla.net/en/ai/uncovering-the-history-of-coins-fascinating-facts-and-stories/

31. United States Mint. (n.d.). Coloring pages. Retrieved from https://kids.usmint.gov/resources/coloring-pages

32. World currencies – Money and Finance. (n.d.). Retrieved from https://www.ducksters.com/money/world_currencies.php